MW00466684

Premillennialism

**Why There Must Be a Future
Earthly Kingdom of Jesus**

Premillennialism

Why There Must Be a Future Earthly Kingdom of Jesus

Michael J. Vlach

Theological Studies Press
Los Angeles, California

© 2015 by Michael J. Vlach

All rights reserved. No portion of this book may be reproduced, stored in a retrieval system, or transmitted in any form or by any means—electronic, mechanical, photocopy, recording, or any other except for brief quotations in printed reviews without the prior permission of the publisher.

Vlach, Michael, 1966 –
Premillennialism / Michael J. Vlach

ISBN-13: 978-0-692-49950-4
ISBN-10: 0-692-49950-4

All Scripture quotations, unless otherwise indicated, are taken from the New American Standard Bible®, Copyright © 1960, 1962, 1963, 1968, 1971, 1972, 1973, 1975, 1977, 1995 by the Lockman Foundation. Used by permission (www.Lockman.org).

Printed in the United States of America

Contents

INTRODUCTION

This book has a narrow purpose. Its aim is to present a positive, biblical case and rationale for premillennialism—the view that there will be a thousand-year reign of Jesus upon the earth after Jesus' second coming but before the Eternal State. This is not a comprehensive discussion of premillennialism or the kingdom of God. There are several historical and biblical issues associated with premillennialism and the kingdom that this work does not cover. Nor is this a full discussion of the rival views of amillennialism and postmillennialism. Doing this would greatly expand the extent of this book. Instead, this book's focus is on key biblical arguments for the premillennial view and reasons why this perspective is true.

Maintaining balance on the millennial issue is important. For most of church history good Christians have disagreed on the millennium, and millennial views should not become barriers of fellowship. On the other hand, the millennium is not some incidental doctrine that doesn't really matter. It is a major part of the Bible's storyline and involves the nature and timing of Jesus' kingdom. The idea of a future earthly kingdom of the Messiah is not something dropped from the sky in Revelation 20. It has deep roots back to Genesis 1.

Sadly, in recent years it has become fashionable to avoid expressing a millennial view or to express how non-important this issue really is. I have read whole-Bible theology books recently that do not even offer a millennial position. But how can one attempt to explain the Bible's storyline and not address the timing and nature of Jesus' messianic, mediatorial, millennial reign? Does it not matter whether Jesus' millennial kingdom reign is now or in the future, spiritual or physical? I think it does. Some think the millennium is a controversial issue that is not that important. But when I think of the millennium I think of the timing and nature of Jesus' kingdom reign. And I want to know what the Bible says on these issues.

The timing and nature of Jesus' millennial reign are important, and the Bible's storyline cannot be accurately grasped unless one gets this issue right. The view presented here is that this present age is an important phase of God's purposes. Jesus has appeared, bringing salvation to all who believe in Him. The church proclaims the kingdom message to a lost world. But there is a coming kingdom reign over this earth to complete and fulfill God's purposes before the Eternal State begins. There must be a successful reign of the Last Adam (Jesus) and His saints from and over the realm where God tasked the first man, Adam, to rule. So the idea of an earthly kingdom where man rules the earth on God's behalf goes back to Genesis 1 where the first man, Adam, was tasked with ruling from and over the earth for the glory of God. When Adam failed God's expectation for a successful earthly reign, this expectation was never revoked (see Psalm 8) but remains unfulfilled throughout history. The return of Jesus with His kingdom will be the fulfillment of the earthly rule God expects. This is where premillennialism brings clarity to the Bible's storyline.

The millennium's timing and nature is the focus of this book. This work's contents will probably be most accessible to those who have some prior knowledge of issues related to the millennium and the debates concerning it. But my hope is that it will be of help to all who want to know what the millennium is and why it is important in God's plans. Jesus will complete God's purposes for this earth, and He will have a sustained and recognized reign in the realm where He was rejected. Thus, the coming millennium should be something all God's people anticipate.

1

THREE MILLENNIAL VIEWS

Legend has it some seminary students once asked their professor for his view of the millennium. Was he a premillennialist, an amillennialist, or a postmillennialist? "None of them," he replied, "I'm panmillennial." The students were confused since they had never heard of such a view. "What's that?" they asked. "Everything will pan out in the end," he wryly declared. This story continues to bring a smile to those who are aware of the ongoing debates concerning the timing of the millennium. But what started as a joke has gained some traction. Some who have tired over the debate have embraced the title of "panmillennialist," affirming an agnostic view of the timing of the millennium. I even came across a book that listed "Panmillennialism" as a millennial view alongside the "Pre," "A," and "Post" views.[1]

The "panmillennial" approach, whether held formally or informally, is sad. It gives the impression that the details of God's plans to restore all things are not that important, at least the millennial phase of it. But events to come are necessary to our Christian worldview. We should be interested in these matters. Would you persevere through three-fourths of a good movie and then leave before the ending? Or how many enjoy a good book but then refuse to read the final chapters? These questions seem silly since the ending matters—a lot. But some Christians are willing to forego God's future plans. They dive deeply into matters related to creation, the

---

[1] Jim Willis and Barbara Willis, *Armageddon Now: The End of the World A to Z* (Canton, MI: Visible Ink Press, 2006), 111.

Fall, and redemption in Christ, but then punt on the timing and nature of Jesus' kingdom. But that is not the right approach. In fact, it is short-sighted.

Premillennialism is the view that there will be a thousand-year kingdom of Jesus after Jesus' second coming but before the Eternal State. This perspective has been well-represented in the last two centuries, particularly in the United States. But the last several decades have brought works promoting amillennialism and postmillennialism. All three views have capable proponents and defenders.

So how does this book attempt to contribute to the discussion? As stated in my introduction, my purpose is to present a scriptural case and rationale for premillennialism. It will address why premillennialism *is true* and why it *must be true*. It also presents a biblical case as to why Jesus' millennial kingdom comes after this present age but before the final Eternal State. This goes beyond focusing solely on Revelation 20, which often dominates discussions on premillennialism. I will address Revelation 20 later, but it is important to grasp that premillennialism is supported by many passages, including several in the Old Testament. It also has connections with the earthly kingdom task given to man in Gen 1:26–28. Premillennialism starts with the beginning of the Bible's story.

While at times this book will interact with the rival positions of amillennialism and postmillennialism, those perspectives are not the primary focus here. Premillennialism is a biblical doctrine that can be proven in a positive manner. The main reason for holding to premillennialism is because the Bible clearly teaches it. The view is not solely dependent on refuting alternative views, although mentioning weaknesses of the other views is helpful to a point. So the focus here will be on a positive case for premillennialism from the Bible.

Also, while not the focus of this book, I acknowledge there are variations within premillennialism, namely the two camps of *dispensational/futuristic premillennialism* and *historic premillennialism*. Both forms of premillennialism affirm an intermediate kingdom of Jesus after the second coming but before the Eternal State. Their primary disagreement concerns how Israel and the church relate to this coming millennial kingdom. Dispensational/futuristic premillennialists believe that Israel is restored as a nation during the millennium with a functional role of leadership and service to other nations during this time (Isa 2:2–4). It affirms that all covenant aspects and promises in the Bible must be fulfilled, including physical promises and national promises to Israel. The fulfillment of God's promises to national Israel coincide with and harmonize with the great blessings He is also bringing to the church. Dispensational premillennialism also rejects all forms of replacement theology in which the church is viewed as the replacement or fulfillment of Israel so that national Israel ceases to have theological significance in God's purposes.

On the other hand, historic premillennialism also affirms a coming earthly kingdom reign of Jesus. But today's historic premillennialists are often less literal with national promises to Israel. Some also assert that Old Testament physical blessings promised to Israel can be fulfilled spiritually in the church. For example, the influential historic premillennialist, George Eldon Ladd (1911–82), declared:

> The Old Testament must be interpreted by the New Testament. In principle it is quite possible that the prophecies addressed originally to literal Israel describing physical blessings have their fulfillment exclusively in the spiritual blessings enjoyed by the church. It is also possible that the Old Testament expectation of a kingdom on earth could be reinterpreted by the New Testament altogether of blessings in the spiritual realm.[2]

Ladd also asserted that the church is the "new Israel."[3]

It should be understood that there are differences of thought among historic premillennialists. Historic premillennialists of the nineteenth and early twentieth centuries at times affirmed a significant place for national Israel in the coming millennial kingdom. For example, Charles Haddon Spurgeon (1834–92) declared, "It is also certain that the Jews, as a people, will yet own Jesus of Nazareth, the Son of David, as their King, and that they will return to their own land." This is in connection with a coming earthly millennial reign when Jesus "will reign amongst his ancients gloriously, and . . . there will be a thousand years of joy and peace such as were never known

---

[2] George E. Ladd, "Revelation 20 and the Millennium," *Review and Expositor* 57 (1960): 167.

[3] George Ladd, *A Theology of the New Testament* (Grand Rapids: Eerdmans 1974), 355, 545.

on this earth before."[4] But many (not all) historic premillennialists of today follow George Ladd in affirming a form of replacement theology in regard to Israel and the church and viewing Old Testament promises to Israel as being spiritualized to the church.

The position of this book is dispensational/futuristic premillennialism since I strongly affirm a coming salvation and restoration of national Israel in complete fulfillment of the eternal covenants and promises of the Old Testament, including their physical and national elements. The New Testament reaffirms the expectation of a restoration of Israel on several occasions—Matt 19:28; 23:37–39; Luke 1:32–33; 21:24; Acts 1:6; Rom 11:26–27; and Rev 7:4–8. Thus, there is a close relationship between the millennium and Israel.

But the reader should note that the debate between the two premillennial camps is not the focus of this book. My attention, instead, concerns whether the Bible teaches a millennial kingdom after the return of Jesus but before the Eternal State. On this issue both dispensational and historic premillennialists stand in agreement. I have benefited from the contributions of historic premillennialists on the millennium while having differences at times with them concerning Israel's role in the millennium.[5]

Millennial Views Defined

Some definitions are needed at this point. The word "millennium" refers to the thousand-year period mentioned seven times in Rev 20:1–7. The term "millennium" itself is not referred to in the Bible. It is a Latin term that means "one-thousand years." *Mille* is a "thousand" and *annum* refers to "year." So "millennium" is a thousand years. In the context of Revelation 20, the millennium is a kingdom reign of Jesus with His saints for a thousand years. Below are definitions of the various millennial views.

---

[4] Charles Haddon Spurgeon, "The Harvest and the Vintage," in *The Metropolitan Tabernacle Pulpit*, 50:553–54. For more information on Spurgeon's views on the millennium see Dennis M. Swanson, "The Millennial Position of Spurgeon," *The Master's Seminary Journal*, 7, no. 2 (Fall 1996): 183–212.

[5] For more on a case for national Israel's future significance and an argument against replacement theology, see my book *Has the Church Replaced Israel?: A Theological Evaluation* (Nashville, TN: B&H Academic, 2010).

Premillennialism

The term "premillennialism" refers to how the thousand-year reign of Jesus relates to the timing of His second coming. The prefix "pre-" means "before" and indicates that Jesus will come before the millennium. Thus, *premillennialism is the view that the thousand-year kingdom mentioned in Revelation 20 follows Jesus' second coming to earth*. For premillennialists, this thousand-year reign of Jesus the Messiah comes between two events—the second coming of Jesus and the Eternal State. This premillennial kingdom is an "intermediate kingdom" since it comes after the present age but before the Eternal State. God's future kingdom, therefore, has a millennial phase and then an eternal kingdom phase.

According to premillennialism, this present age is not the final phase of God's kingdom and covenant plan. Many spiritual blessings have been poured out on Christians in this age, such as a new heart and the indwelling Holy Spirit. But several national and physical blessings still need to be fulfilled. Much has happened in this age, but more is to come.

Also, when the millennial kingdom is established after Jesus returns to earth, Satan will be imprisoned and his activities will completely cease for a thousand years (see Rev 20:1–3). The saints of God will be rewarded and vindicated for their faithful service during this present age, which is characterized by persecution from the world and Satan. They then will reign over the nations during the millennial era (see Rev 20:4). After this millennial kingdom, Satan will be released for a short time to lead a rebellion at the "beloved city" of Jerusalem, but he is defeated and sentenced to the lake of fire forever (see Rev 20:7–10). Then the Eternal State will begin after all God's enemies and death have been finally defeated.

Another important aspect of premillennialism is the belief that the resurrection of the dead will occur in two phases. The first is a physical resurrection of believers to participate in Jesus' millennial kingdom. The second is a physical resurrection of unbelievers who will be sentenced to the lake of fire (see Rev 20:4–5). This position of premillennialism is in contrast to amillennialism and postmillennialism, which we will now define.

Amillennialism

Amillennialism asserts that the millennium of Revelation 20 is being fulfilled spiritually now between the two comings of Jesus Christ. Christ is reigning in His millennial kingdom now. Variations exist concerning where and how this reign occurs. Some have held that the church is the kingdom on earth, while other amillennialists have claimed that the millennium is the reign of Jesus and the saints in heaven during this age.[6] This latter view in particular removes Jesus' millennial kingdom from having an earthly influence.

Also, according to amillennialism, Satan is currently restrained in his ability to deceive the nations but he is still active. While Christ's kingdom is in operation this world will continue to deteriorate until Jesus comes again. The millennium will end with Jesus' second coming. Then there will be one general resurrection and judgment for believers and unbelievers and then the Eternal State will begin.

Amillennialism affirms that Jesus' millennial kingdom is *now* in timing and *spiritual* in nature. This millennial kingdom coincides with Jesus' messianic/Davidic reign. This contrasts with the premillennial view that Jesus' millennial kingdom is future and earthly. Amillennialism is also based on the belief that this present age is the culmination of God's kingdom and covenant program before the Eternal State. For them, Jesus' kingdom is in full operation now.

Premillennialism, not amillennialism, was the predominant view in the first two hundred years of church history. However, the early church did evidence hints of what later would become amillennialism. For example, Origen (185–254) popularized the allegorical approach to interpreting Scripture, and in doing so, laid a hermeneutical basis for amillennialism and its view that the promised kingdom of Christ was spiritual and not earthly in nature. Eusebius (A.D. 270–340), an associate of the emperor Constantine the Great (A.D. 272–337), viewed Constantine's reign as the messianic banquet and held to anti-premillennial views. Tyconius, an African Donatist of the

---

[6] One example is Sam Storms who says, ". . . I am now persuaded that Revelation 20:4–6 is concerned exclusively with *the experience of the martyrs in the intermediate state.*" Sam Storms, *Kingdom Come: The Amillennial Alternative* (Geanies House, Fearn, Ross-Shire, Scotland, UK: Christian Focus Publications, 2013), 451. Emphases in original. He also says, ". . . in Revelation 20 he [John] . . . describes the intermediate state as *souls living and reigning with Christ.*" (461). Emphases in original.

fourth century, was one of the earliest theologians to challenge premillennialism. He rejected the futuristic view of Revelation 20. He also viewed the first resurrection of Rev 20:4 as a spiritual resurrection which was the new birth. Augustine of Hippo (354–430), who is often referred to as the "Father of Amillennialism," popularized the views of Tyconius. Augustine abandoned premillennialism partly because of what he considered to be the excesses and carnalities of this view. Augustine identified the church in its visible form with the kingdom of God. For him, the millennial rule of Christ was taking place in and through the church. His book, *City of God*, was significant in the promotion and acceptance of amillennialism. Augustine's amillennialism quickly became the accepted view of the church. Amillennialism soon became the prevailing doctrine of the Roman Catholic Church and is still held by many today.[7]

Postmillennialism

Postmillennialism claims the millennium of Revelation 20 will be fulfilled between the two comings of Christ as Jesus' kingdom starts small and eventually permeates all areas of society, Christianizing the world. Through the reign of Jesus from heaven and the Holy Spirit-blessed gospel, the kingdom of God will start small but increasingly grows, spreads, and becomes the dominant influence in the world. During this millennial era, Satan is restrained in his ability to deceive the nations but he is still active. When the gospel has triumphed over all areas of society then Jesus will return. Then there will be one general resurrection and judgment for both believers and unbelievers and then the Eternal State will begin.

Postmillennialists offer several lines of support. The psalms and prophecies from the Old Testament that describe prosperous and peaceful conditions on earth are taken as evidence for a millennium before the return of Jesus (Isa 65:17–25; Psalm 72). The Great Commission of Matt 28:19–20 is understood as the vehicle for the transformation of the nations. In addition, the parables of the mustard seed and leaven (Matt 13:31–33) show a gradual yet large growth of the kingdom after a small beginning.

---

[7] For a thorough and academic defense of amillennialism see Sam Storms, *Kingdom Come*; Anthony A. Hoekema, *The Bible and the Future* (Grand Rapids: Eerdmans, 1994); Kim Riddlebarger, *A Case for Amillennialism: Understanding the End Times* (Grand Rapids: Baker, 2013).

Both amillennialism and postmillennialism believe that the millennium occurs in this present age between the two comings of Jesus and that the second coming of Jesus brings an end to the millennium and ushers in the Eternal State. The millennium is not a kingdom that comes as a result of Jesus' second coming, but it is a kingdom reign that occurs between His two comings. Where postmillennialists and amillennialists differ concerns the nature of the present kingdom. Amillennialists hold that world conditions will deteriorate until the coming of Jesus. Postmillennialists, on the other hand, believe that the gospel will transform the world in all ways before the return of Jesus. When Jesus returns, He comes back to a world that has been won over by the gospel.[8]

Conclusion

With these definitions in mind we now turn to our main issue. Is premillennialism biblical? The following chapters will discuss a biblical presentation and rationale for premillennialism. Revelation 20 tells us that the time period for the kingdom of Jesus is a thousand years. But the concept of an earthly messianic kingdom is found in both the Old and New Testaments. While some claim that premillennialism can only be supported by Revelation 20, it is supported in other passages. Premillennialism is rooted in the Old Testament and stated in a New Testament book (Revelation) that is explicitly prophetic in its genre and gives chronological details concerning things to come. Premillennialism is based on a consistent application of historical-grammatical hermeneutics, which takes into account the genre and literary structure of the books of the Bible, along with canonical developments regarding the kingdom program. And it is compatible with multiple Bible passages that place the kingdom reign of Christ with His second coming to earth (Matt 19:28; 25:31). It is a position consistent with the biblical worldview which affirms the goodness of God's creation and the restoration of all things material and immaterial (see Col 1:15–20). It is also consistent with the storyline of the Bible that the Last Adam must have a successful reign from and over the realm—earth—where the first Adam failed.

---

[8] For a defense of postmillennialism see Kenneth L. Gentry, Jr., "Postmillennialism," in *Three Views on the Millennium and Beyond*, ed. Darrell L. Bock (Grand Rapids: Zondervan, 1999), 13–57.

2

ROOTS OF AN EARTHLY KINGDOM
IN THE OLD TESTAMENT

This chapter begins the case that premillennialism has its roots in the Old Testament and that the millennial kingdom mentioned in Revelation 20 is buoyed by information in the Old and New Testaments. Overall, this case involves:

1. The kingdom mandate of Gen 1:26–28.

2. Old Testament passages that predict a coming earthly kingdom under the presence of the Messiah.

3. Old Testament passages that predict an intermediate kingdom with conditions better than the present age but not perfect like the Eternal State.

4. New Testament predictions of a future earthly kingdom.

5. An earthly, intermediate kingdom of a thousand years found in Rev 20:1–6.

The following chart shows these connections:

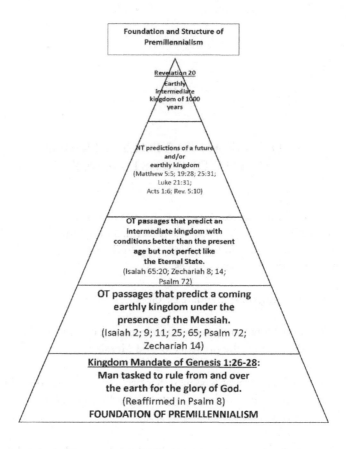

So the roots of an earthly kingdom begin in Genesis 1. While this passage does not mention a "thousand years," it explains the importance of man's rule over the earth. God created a beautiful and wonderful world in six days. With Gen 1:26–28, God made man in His image and gave Adam an earthly kingdom task:

> Then God said, "Let Us make man in Our image, according to Our likeness; and <u>let them rule over the fish of the sea and over the birds of the sky and over the cattle and over all the earth, and over every creeping thing that creeps on the earth</u>." God created man in His own image, in the image of God He created him; male and female He created them. God blessed them; and

God said to them, "Be fruitful and multiply, and fill the earth, and subdue it; and rule over the fish of the sea and over the birds of the sky and over every living thing that moves on the earth" (Gen 1:26–28; emphases added).

This reveals a strong connection between man and earth. God made man in His image and instructs him to rule over the earth and its creatures. This connection is further explained in the detailed account of man's creation in Genesis 2 where God formed man from the dust of the ground (see Gen 2:7). The Hebrew word for "man" is *adam* and the term for "ground" is *adamah*. The close connection between *adam* and *adamah* emphasizes the relationship between man and the ground he is to rule over.

God instructs man to "rule" over the creation. The Hebrew term for "rule," which is used twice in Gen 1:26–28, is *rādāh* and means "have dominion," "rule," or "dominate."[1] The term is used later of the Messiah's future reign in Ps 110:2: "The LORD will stretch forth Your strong scepter from Zion, *saying*, "Rule [*rādāh*] in the midst of Your enemies."

The word for "subdue" is the Hebrew term *kābaš*, which means "dominate" or "bring into bondage."[2] The term "especially speaks of the work of a king (e.g., 2 Sam. 8:11)."[3] Both verbs "rule" and "subdue" are linked to dominion and show, as Merrill observes, that "man is created to reign in a manner that demonstrates his lordship, his domination (by force if necessary) over all creation."[4] This is evident with man's naming of the animals, which was a demonstration of dominion (see Gen 2:19–20). Thus, there is a royal and kingly aspect to the language of Gen 1:26–28.

The *realm* of this kingdom rule for man is the earth, not heaven. As Ps 115:16 declares, "The heavens are the LORD's, but the earth

---

[1] See Francis Brown, S. R. Driver, and Charles A. Briggs, *A Hebrew and English Lexicon of the Old Testament* (Oxford: Clarendon, 1962), 921.

[2] The term is used for subduing the land of Canaan so it could provide for the people of Israel. See Num 32:22, 29 and Josh 18:1.

[3] Peter J. Gentry and Stephen J. Wellum, *Kingdom through Covenant: A Biblical-Theological Understanding of the Covenants* (Wheaton, IL: Crossway, 2012), 196.

[4] Eugene H. Merrill, "A Theology of the Pentateuch," in *A Biblical Theology of the Old Testament*, ed. Roy B. Zuck (Chicago: Moody Press, 1991), 15.

He has given to the human race." So the kingdom is an earthly kingdom, with Adam established as its king. God did not create Adam and mankind to rule heaven or to rule earth from heaven. Man is to rule *from* and *over* the earth with "an earthly vocation."[5] In addition to his relationship with God, Adam possessed physical and social/political authority. This was to manifest itself in every area— agriculture, architecture, domestication of animals, harnessing of energy and natural resources, and other areas.[6] As Middleton notes, "the human creature is made to worship God in a distinctive way: by interacting with the earth, using our God-given power to transform our earthly environment into a complex world (a sociocultural world) that glorifies our creator."[7]

Psalm 8, which functions like a restatement or commentary on Gen 1:26–28, also reveals man's relationship to the creation:

> What is man that You take thought of him,
> And the son of man that You care for him?
> Yet You have made him a little lower than God,
> And You crown him with glory and majesty!
> You make him to rule over the works of Your hands;
> You have put all things under his feet,
> All sheep and oxen,
> And also the beasts of the field,
> The birds of the heavens and the fish of the sea,
> Whatever passes through the paths of the seas (Ps 8:4–8).

The connection with Gen 1:26–28 in Ps 8:4–8 is clear.[8] In Genesis 1 Adam was created in God's image so that he could serve God

---

[5] J. Richard Middleton, *A New Heaven and a New Earth: Reclaiming Biblical Eschatology* (Grand Rapids: Baker, 2014), 39.

[6] See Wayne Grudem, *Politics According to the Bible: A Comprehensive Resource for Understanding Modern Political Issues in Light of Scripture* (Grand Rapids: Zondervan, 2010), 325. Grudem says, "God expected Adam and Eve and their descendants to explore and develop the earth's resources in such a way that they would bring benefit to themselves and other human beings."

[7] Middleton, 41.

[8] Psalm 8 could be viewed as a commentary on Gen 1:26–28. ". . . vv. 5–8 parallel the Gen. 1 story of God's making men and women godlike and giving them power over the rest of the animate world." John Goldingay, *Psalms: Volume*

by ruling and subduing the creation on God's behalf for God's glory. Psalm 8 shows that man still possesses the right to rule the creation. David writes thousands of years later in a fallen world still under the devastating effects of the curse. Yet a marred world has not removed man's right to rule. It is not the case that with the Fall God changes his plans and makes man's ultimate destiny heaven as opposed to earth.

The truths of Ps 8:6 concerning all things being placed under man's feet will be picked up by Paul in 1 Cor 15:25–28 and Eph 1:22 and with the writer of Hebrews in Heb 2:5–8. With Eph 1:22 Jesus' resurrection and ascension are the reasons for God's putting "all things in subjection under His feet." So the authority to rule the earth is granted to Jesus by the Father and will be exercised by Jesus when He comes again (see Ps 110:1–2).[9]

With 1 Cor 15:25–27 Paul quotes Ps 8:6 regarding Jesus' coming earthly reign. The writer of Hebrews also quotes Ps 8:6 to reaffirm that man still has the right to rule the earth although all things are not subjected to man in this age (Heb 2:5–8). These passages indicate that the fulfillment of Psalm 8, which is drawing upon Gen 1:26–28, will occur in a world to come in connection with the ultimate Man, Jesus, the Last Adam (see 1 Cor 15:24–28; 45).

So how do these passages relate to Genesis 1? Genesis 1 teaches that man was created to rule from and over the earth on God's behalf. Although he is fallen and unable to accomplish this task on his own, ruling the earth is still man's destiny, as Psalm 8 and Heb 2:5–8 reveal. So man's kingly right is earthly since he is a creature placed on earth to rule from and over the earth. The millennial kingdom will highlight the successful reign of the Last Adam (1 Cor 15:45) in the reign where the first Adam was tasked but failed. When Jesus comes again He will share this reign with those who identify with Him (see Rev 2:26–27; 3:21; 20:4). While Jesus is the ultimate King (Rev 11:15), His followers are also a "kingdom" and "they will reign upon the earth" (Rev 5:10).

1: *Psalms 1–41*, in Baker Commentary on the Old Testament Wisdom and Psalms (Grand Rapids: Baker, 2006), 159.

[9] This could be similar to the parable of the nobleman in Luke 19:11–27 where Jesus likened Himself to a nobleman who needed to travel to a distant country to receive the rights to a kingdom and then return. Once the rights are given he then returns to rule, rewarding his servants and destroying his enemies.

In this way, the mediatorial reign of man on earth is fulfilled. Adam failed but success will occur with the ultimate Man, Jesus, who not only successfully reigns, He shares His reign with His people. This is corporate representation at its best. As Jesus succeeds, His people succeed. This kingdom reign then transitions into the Eternal State. There, both the Father and Jesus are on the throne in the New Jerusalem (Rev 22:3), and the saints reign forever over the New Earth (Rev 22:5). A successful mediatorial reign leads to an eternal reign in the eternal kingdom. As shown below:

Mediatorial Kingdom Connections

Gen 1:26–28 (unfallen creation)
Man tasked to rule
from and over the earth
↓
Psalm 8 (fallen world)
(explains Gen 1:26–28)
Even in a fallen world, man still
possesses right to rule over the earth
↓
Heb 2:5–8 (fallen world)
(quotes Psalm 8:6)
Man still possesses the right
to rule the earth but this is not
occurring in this age
↓
Eph 1:22 (Heaven)
(quotes Psalm 8:6)
With ascension Jesus possesses
right to rule the earth
↓
1 Cor 15:26 (Millennial Kingdom)
(quotes Psalm 8:6)
Jesus as ultimate Man ("Last Adam") will fulfill
man's mandate to rule the earth after His return
↓
Rev 2:26–27; 3:21; 5:10 (Millennial Kingdom)
Jesus will share His rule over the
earth with those who identity with Him
in the millennial kingdom
↓
Rev 22:3, 5 (Eternal State)
God and Jesus are on the throne and
the saints reign forever in the Eternal State

Kingdom Failure in the Old Testament

Genesis 3 reveals that man disobeyed God and death followed. The rupture in man's relationship with God sent massive ripples throughout all of creation. Man's sin also meant failure of the kingdom mandate of Gen 1:26–28. Man cannot fulfill his destiny while severed from his Creator. Instead of ruling the earth successfully, man himself would be swallowed up by the ground as he returns to the ground as dust (see Gen 3:19). The list of those who died in Genesis 5 testifies that man does not successfully rule nature, instead the earth swallows him up as he returns to dust.

The account of Noah's flood confirms that man's thoughts and deeds are only evil (Gen 6:5) and that global judgment was necessary (Genesis 6–8). The Tower of Babel incident shows man continued to rebel against God's intent for him to multiply over the earth, wanting to establish a kingdom and name for themselves (Gen 11:1–9). The list of nations and people groups in Genesis 10–11 highlights that God is sovereign over the nations and where they reside. It also shows that these nations matter to God and God has a plan for them.

Genesis 12 begins an important phase of God's plan to establish His kingdom on earth. God will raise up Israel through the descendants of Abraham, Isaac, and Jacob, and then through the twelve sons of Jacob and the many descendants from them. The developing Hebrew people would function as the nucleus for God's coming kingdom. Yet the slavery of this people in Egypt posed an obstacle to God's plans. The descendants of Abraham, Isaac, and Jacob were intended to be a blessing to all nations (Gen 12:3; 22:18), but this could not happen if this people remained forever enslaved in Egypt.

After the exodus from Egypt, at Mount Sinai, God told the Israelites they would be "a kingdom of priests and a holy nation" (Exod 19:6). If Israel obeyed the commands of the Mosaic Covenant then they would be a witness to the nations of the greatness of God (Deut 4:5–6). This earthly kingdom seemed to be on the brink of success in 1 Kings 8–10 under the reign of Solomon when the promises of land, seed, and universal blessings of the Abrahamic Covenant (see Gen 12:2–3) seemed well on their way to fulfillment. Israel had many descendants, the land borders were large, and Gentile powers were coming to seek the wisdom of Israel's king—Solomon.

But a permanent, successful earthly kingdom would not occur at this time. First Kings 11 details the tragic disobedience of Solomon which led the nation of Israel on a trajectory toward disobedience, division, and dispersion. The Assyrian and Babylonian captivities of Israel showed that Israel's kingdom was a failure because of Israel's stubborn disobedience. There would be returns to the land after captivity, but under the authority of Gentile powers. Israel had entered what Jesus would later refer to as "the times of the Gentiles" (Luke 21:24).

A Future Earthly Kingdom in the Old Testament Prophets

The demise of Israel's kingdom did not mean an end to God's plans to establish an earthly kingdom. While the monarchy deteriorated and then ended in Israel, the prophets arose with a message of a coming, glorious earthly kingdom under the Messiah. With Isa 2:2–4 the prophet Isaiah predicts a coming kingdom with Jerusalem as the capital city and nations streaming to this city to know the ways of God. The Lord will judge between the nations and make righteous decisions on behalf of them. This is a time of international harmony as weapons for warfare are no longer needed. Such conditions of an earthly kingdom with international harmony have never occurred in history yet, but they await the coming kingdom of Jesus the Messiah. Isaiah 9:6–7 predicts that a "child" and "son" (Jesus) will be born and "the government shall be upon his shoulder" and of His kingdom "there will be no end."

Isaiah 11 tells of a time when a righteous descendant of Jesse (i.e. Jesus) (Isa 11:1) will "decide with fairness for the afflicted of the earth" (11:4). Isaiah 65:17–25 predicts a future time when houses will be built and agriculture will blossom, and those who labor well will reap the benefits of their hard work. The animal kingdom will exist in harmony. With Psalm 2, David tells of a coming day when God will establish His King upon Mount Zion in Jerusalem, where He will rule the nations in the realm where they once rebelled against God. Psalm 72 predicts a time when a righteous Davidic King will "rule from sea to sea . . . from the River to the ends of the earth" (Ps 72:8). "All nations will serve him" (72:11). This King will "deliver the needy" and the "afflicted" (72:12). He will also "have compassion on the poor and the needy" (72:13). During this time there will be "abundance of grain in the earth on top of the mountains" (72:16). These depictions cannot be spiritualized or allegorized to purely spiritual blessings, nor can these be fulfilled with the church. These anticipate conditions in a coming earthly kingdom.

Daniel 2 declares that a divine "stone" from heaven will dramatically shatter the Gentile kingdoms of the world and grow to fill the whole earth, which means an earthly kingdom (Dan 2:31–45). Zechariah 14 also tells of a time when the Lord will return to the Mount of Olives and be King over all the earth, including its nations.

These passages reveal a coming earthly kingdom of God under the Messiah. No indication exists that these promises of earthly kingdom won't be literally fulfilled, or that these promises will eventually give way to spiritual realities. Nor is there any indication that these passages should be spiritualized to this present age with the church.

3

THE KINGDOM THAT FOLLOWS TRIBULATION

Precursors of the Coming Kingdom

Premillennialism asserts that the millennial kingdom of the Messiah follows certain conditions such as the Day of the Lord, global tribulation, cosmic signs, the return of Jesus, and other events. The millennium does not exist before or run concurrently with these events but comes into existence after them. For example, when Jesus predicted cataclysmic events in Luke 21, like cosmic signs and roaring waves, He pointed to these and said, "So you also, when you see these things happening recognize that the kingdom of God is near" (Luke 21:31). According to Jesus, certain events will indicate that the kingdom is on the brink of arrival. The Bible teaches that Jesus' messianic, millennial reign follows certain events and does not come before them. The passages below illustrate this point.

Isaiah 24–25

One passage where we see global tribulation before kingdom is Isaiah 24–25. This section comes within Isaiah 24–27 which is one of the most significant prophetic passages in the Old Testament. It is sometimes referred to as "Isaiah's Little Apocalypse" since it gives detailed information concerning events to come and is a microcosm for events in the book of Revelation. Our focus here is on chapters 24 and 25 where the pattern of *tribulation before kingdom* is evident.

Isaiah 24:1–20 details a great tribulation coming upon the entire earth and its inhabitants.[1] Verse 1 declares: "Behold, the LORD lays the earth waste, devastates it, distorts its surface and scatters its inhabitants." Verses 5–6 indicate that this time of catastrophic global judgment is because of man's sin:

> The earth is also polluted by its inhabitants, for they transgressed laws, violated statutes, broke the everlasting covenant. Therefore, a curse devours the earth, and those who live in it are held guilty. Therefore, the inhabitants of the earth are burned, and few men are left.

This speaks of global tribulation upon the people of the earth who have transgressed God's standards. But not only are the earth-dwellers facing judgment, planet earth itself is reeling during this period:

> The earth is broken asunder,
> The earth is split through,
> The earth is shaken violently.
> The earth reels to and fro like a drunkard
> And it totters like a shack (Isa 24:19–20b).

So not only are the people of the earth undergoing divine wrath, the planet itself experiences the ramifications of God's judgments. The time of global tribulation also involves judgment on wicked spiritual and earthly forces:

> So it will happen in that day,
> That the LORD will punish the host of heaven on high,
> And the kings of the earth on earth.
> They will be gathered together
> Like prisoners in the dungeon,
> And will be confined in prison;
> And after many days they will be punished (Isa 24:21–22).

---

[1] That this chapter is referring to a global judgment is also clear from the fact that Isaiah 13–23 discusses the nations of the earth and 24:13 states, "For thus it will be in the midst of the earth among the peoples."

But tribulation and judgment are then followed by kingdom conditions, as Isa 25:6–8 reveals:

> The LORD of hosts will prepare a lavish banquet for all peoples on this mountain;
> A banquet of aged wine, choice pieces with marrow,
> And refined, aged wine.
> And on this mountain He will swallow up the covering which is over all peoples,
> Even the veil which is stretched over all nations.
> He will swallow up death for all time,
> And the Lord GOD will wipe tears away from all faces,
> And He will remove the reproach of His people from all the earth;
> For the LORD has spoken.

The "banquet" imagery of chapter 25 refers to God's kingdom (see Matt 8:11). And the events described here follow the tribulation and judgment previously discussed in chapter 24. Thus, Isaiah 24–25 reveals the following chronology: global tribulation, *then* judgment, *then* kingdom. This pattern is found in other passages as well.

Daniel 12:1–3

In Dan 12:1–3 we again see the pattern of tribulation, judgment, and then kingdom:

> Now at that time Michael, the great prince who stands guard over the sons of your people, will arise. And there will be a time of distress such as never occurred since there was a nation until that time; and at that time your people, everyone who is found written in the book, will be rescued. Many of those who sleep in the dust of the ground will awake, these to everlasting life, but the others to disgrace and everlasting contempt. Those who have insight will shine brightly like the brightness of the expanse of heaven, and those who lead the many to righteousness, like the stars forever and ever.

Daniel 12:1 tells of an unparalleled "time of distress" that will come upon Daniel's people, Israel. This is not like previous periods of persecution and tribulation, but a unique period that has "never occurred" before. Verse 2 then tells of the judgment of the righteous and the wicked. Verse 3 then states that those who belong to God "will shine brightly like the brightness of the expanse of heaven, and those who lead the many to righteousness, like the stars forever and ever." This is a reference to the blessings of the kingdom of God. In Matt 13:43, Jesus quoted Dan 12:3 in reference to the righteous at the end of the age who will enter His kingdom. Thus, with Dan 12:1–3 we see the pattern of tribulation ("time of distress") *then* judgment *then* kingdom. Or put another way:

> 12:1: Tribulation
> 12:2: Judgment
> 12:3: Kingdom

Zechariah 14

Zechariah 14 is another major passage that discusses future events. Here we see that the kingdom of God follows tribulation, cosmic signs, the rescue of God's people, and judgment of God's enemies. The first three verses detail a siege of Jerusalem by the nations:

> Behold, a day is coming for the LORD when the spoil taken from you will be divided among you. For I will gather all the nations against Jerusalem to battle, and the city will be captured, the houses plundered, the women ravished and half of the city exiled, but the rest of the people will not be cut off from the city. Then the LORD will go forth and fight against those nations, as when He fights on a day of battle (14:1–3).

This is a future time of tribulation for Israel as the city is under siege by Gentile powers.[2] Verse 4 then discusses the return of the Lord to the Mount of Olives:

---

[2] That this section was not fulfilled in A.D. 70 with the Roman destruction of Jerusalem is clear by the fact that Zechariah 14 predicts the rescue of Jerusalem by the Lord who physically comes to the Mount of Olives near Jerusalem. Jerusalem was not delivered, nor did the Lord physically return to the Mount of Olives in A.D. 70. Plus, the changes to the land discussed in Zechariah 14 have not occurred.

In that day His feet will stand on the Mount of Olives, which is
in front of Jerusalem on the east; and the Mount of Olives will
be split in its middle from east to west by a very large valley, so
that half of the mountain will move toward the north and the
other half toward the south.

Note that the Lord comes to the Mount of Olives in front of
Jerusalem. This is a literal arrival on earth that brings topographical
changes to the area. As the siege of Jerusalem is occurring, things
look bleak for its Jewish inhabitants before the Lord physically
comes to rescue the city. But then He comes to the rescue. The return of the Lord is also connected with cosmic signs:

In that day there will be no light; the luminaries will dwindle.
For it will be a unique day which is known to the LORD, neither
day nor night, but it will come about that at evening time there
will be light (14:6–7).

Zechariah 14:9 then tells of the kingdom of God: "And the
LORD will be king over all the earth; in that day the LORD will be the
only one, and His name the only one."

Put together, these verses show that the Lord's kingdom comes
after a time of tribulation and the Lord's return to earth. When the
King reigns, He reigns "over all the earth." Thus, there is a worldwide earthly kingdom. The earthly kingdoms that were warring
against Jerusalem on earth are now displaced by God's kingdom in
the same realm. God's kingdom does not run concurrently with rebellion on the earth, but comes and dramatically replaces it with a
divine kingdom.

Verse 12 then describes judgment for the enemies of God at
this time: "Now this will be the plague with which the LORD will
strike all the peoples who have gone to war against Jerusalem; their
flesh will rot while they stand on their feet, and their eyes will rot in
their sockets, and their tongue will rot in their mouth." Those who
survive this judgment are then allowed to participate in the kingdom
that is centered in Jerusalem: "Then it will come about that any who
are left of all the nations that went against Jerusalem will go up from
year to year to worship the King, the LORD of hosts, and to celebrate
the Feast of Booths."

In sum, with Zechariah 14, a chronology of events is established: (1) tribulation for Israel; (2) a rescue of God's people; (3) return of the Lord to earth; (4) cosmic signs; (5) judgment; and then (6) kingdom.

Matthew 24–25

When one shifts to the New Testament, the pattern of tribulation before kingdom is repeated. This reveals great continuity with the Old Testament revelation on this topic. The kingdom of God follows events such as the tribulation, cosmic signs, a rescue of God's people, and judgment. For example, in Matthew's account of the Olivet Discourse, Jesus described events connected with His coming that are similar to those found in the Old Testament. In 24:4–28 Jesus described a coming time of "tribulation" (v. 9). This will include false christs, wars, rumors of wars, famines, and plagues (4–8). It also will include persecution of God's people (9–13). This period is also marked by the abomination of desolation that was spoken of by Daniel the prophet (15–22; cf. Dan 9:27). Jesus then detailed cosmic signs, His own coming, and the rescue of His people that will occur immediately after this Tribulation period:

> But immediately after the tribulation of those days THE SUN WILL BE DARKENED, AND THE MOON WILL NOT GIVE ITS LIGHT, AND THE STARS WILL FALL from the sky, and the powers of the heavens will be shaken. And then the sign of the Son of Man will appear in the sky, and then all the tribes of the earth will mourn, and they will see the SON OF MAN COMING ON THE CLOUDS OF THE SKY with power and great glory. And He will send forth His angels with A GREAT TRUMPET and THEY WILL GATHER TOGETHER His elect from the four winds, from one end of the sky to the other (29–31).

Note the chronology. Jesus described a unique time of tribulation that is followed by cosmic signs, His own return, and the rescue of God's people. Matthew 25:31–46 is also significant in that Jesus described the judgment of the nations that will take place after His return to earth and just prior to the establishment of the kingdom of God. Particularly significant are verses 31–34 which state:

But when the Son of Man comes in His glory, and all the angels with Him, then He will sit on His glorious throne. All the nations will be gathered before Him; and He will separate them from one another, as the shepherd separates the sheep from the goats; and He will put the sheep on His right, and the goats on the left. Then the King will say to those on His right, "Come, you who are blessed of My Father, inherit the kingdom prepared for you from the foundation of the world."

Jesus comes in glory with His angels and *then* He sits on "His glorious throne." This is the glorious coming of Jesus from heaven to earth to sit on the Davidic throne (see Luke 1:32–33). It is at His second coming to earth when He assumes the Davidic throne and reigns fully as Messiah on earth. Jesus does not claim He is sitting on the throne of David before He returns to earth.

At this time of Jesus' coming in glory and His assumption of the Davidic throne "all the nations" are "gathered before Him" (v. 32). This is a judgment of the nations that was predicted in Joel 3:12. Unbelievers are referred to as "goats" and believers as "sheep." These are separated from each other and they enter different destinies. The reward and destiny of the righteous sheep is the kingdom—"Come, you who are blessed of My Father, inherit the kingdom prepared for you. . . ." (34). Note that the sheep were not in the kingdom of God before Jesus returned in glory or before the Tribulation period. Instead, the sheep enter the kingdom *after* the Tribulation, *after* Jesus' return, and *after* the sheep/goat judgment. The judgment of the nations precedes the kingdom of God.

Note the chronology of events according to Matthew 24–25:

- Tribulation
- Cosmic signs
- Return of Jesus
- Judgment
- Inheriting of the kingdom

With Luke's account of the Olivet Discourse, the chronology is similar to Matthew 24–25. Luke 21:25–28 states:

"There will be signs in sun and moon and stars, and on the earth dismay among nations, in perplexity at the roaring of the sea and the waves, men fainting from fear and the expectation of the things which are coming upon the world; for the powers of the heavens will be shaken. Then they will see THE SON OF MAN COMING IN A CLOUD with power and great glory. But when these things begin to take place, straighten up and lift up your heads, because your redemption is drawing near."

Jesus described cosmic signs and "dismay among nations." Then the Son of Man comes in power and glory. Also significant is Luke 21:29–31 where Jesus likened the events of the Tribulation with a fig tree and its leaves and what this meant for the nearness of the kingdom of God:

> Then He told them a parable: "Behold the fig tree and all the trees; as soon as they put forth leaves, you see it and know for yourselves that summer is now near. So you also, <u>when you see these things happening, recognize that the kingdom of God is near</u>."

When Jesus said, "When you see these things happening," He was referring to the coming Tribulation events He just described. It is the events of the Tribulation that indicate that "the kingdom of God is near." The kingdom does not run during or before the Tribulation—it follows it. There are Tribulation events and then the kingdom comes. The dramatic events of the Tribulation period mean the kingdom's establishment is near but not yet arrived. But tribulation will give way to Christ's kingdom.

This same pattern of tribulation and judgment before kingdom is found in the book of Revelation. Chapters 6–18 describe dramatic events in a Tribulation that is followed by the second coming of Jesus, the judgment of God's enemies including Satan (19:11–20:1–3) and the reign of the saints with Jesus in His millennial kingdom (20:4–6).

Later we will go into more detail on the millennial kingdom in the book of Revelation. But the testimony of both the Old and New Testaments is that certain conditions occur before the Messiah's reign on earth. These conditions are tribulation, cosmic signs, rescue of God's people, and judgment of God's enemies.

4

PRECURSORS OF THE MILLENNIUM
IN THE OLD TESTAMENT

In his defense of amillennialism, theologian Robert B. Strimple referred to the concept of "one-text premillennialists"—those who allegedly rely solely on Rev 20:1–10 for their view that there will be an earthly kingdom of Christ after the second coming of Jesus.[1] There is a common perception that premillennialism is based solely on Revelation 20 and without this passage premillennialism would have no biblical support. But the concept of an earthly kingdom after the return of Christ but before the Eternal State is consistent with Old Testament prophetic passages. While Revelation 20 is the most explicit passage discussing an intermediate kingdom, several passages in the Old Testament support this idea as well. In discussing this point we will see two things. First, Isaiah 24–25 is a backdrop for what is described in Revelation 19 and 20. And second, there are passages that suggest an era of time that is different from our present era but also different from the time of the Eternal State.

---

[1] Robert B. Strimple, "Amillennialism," in *Three Views on the Millennium and Beyond*, ed. Darrell L. Bock (Grand Rapids: Zondervan, 1999), 118. Strimple was mostly referring to George Ladd. We are not claiming that Strimple is saying that all premillennialists claim they have only one passage to support premillennialism. George Ladd declared, "A millennial doctrine cannot be based on Old Testament prophecies but should be based on the New Testament alone. . . . The only place in the Bible that speaks of an actual millennium is the passage in Revelation 20:1–6." "Historic Premillennialism," in *The Meaning of the Millennium: Four Views*, ed. Robert G. Clouse (Downers Grove, IL: InterVarsity Press, 1977), 32.

Isaiah 24–25 and Revelation 19–20

The book of Revelation is based on revelations given to the apostle John. John sees prophetic symbols and circumstances that reveal God's plans. Yet what John sees corresponds with earlier revelation from the Old Testament. Beale and McDonough are correct that, "The OT in general plays such a major role that a proper understanding of its use is necessary for an adequate view of Revelation as a whole."[2] Isaiah in general, and Isaiah's Little Apocalypse of chapters 24–27 in particular, have a strong connection with Revelation. Isaiah's Little Apocalypse is a major backdrop and part of the informing theology for events of the book of Revelation, including its discussion of a millennial kingdom.

Isaiah 24:1–20 and Global Judgment

Earlier we discussed the chronology of Isaiah 24–25 in which the kingdom follows worldwide tribulation. Here we visit Isaiah 24–27 to show how this section is a backdrop for the millennium of Revelation 20. But first the context must be established. Isaiah 9:6 predicted that a "son" would come and that "the government will rest on His shoulders." This is a reference to the coming Messiah we now know as Jesus. Chapters 13–23 then discuss God's plans for the nations of the earth. Then Isaiah 24–27 addresses God's plans to judge the nations and set up His kingdom on the earth. Isaiah 24:1–20 describes a time of terrible tribulation for the earth and its inhabitants. Verse 1 summarizes the chapter: "Behold, the LORD lays the earth waste, devastates it, distorts its surface and scatters its inhabitants." This is not a localized judgment on the land of Israel but universal judgment. The entire earth and its inhabitants are in view here. As Grogan states concerning chapter 24:

> This chapter is fundamental to the three that follow it. It speaks of a judgment that is universal. Not only does it make no reference to particular nations or specific historical events, it does

---

[2] G. K. Beale and Sean M. McDonough, "Revelation," in *Commentary on the New Testament Use of the Old Testament*, eds. G. K. Beale and D. A. Carson (Grand Rapids: Baker, 2007), 1082. These authors note that Isaiah is the most used Old Testament book in Revelation (1082). Beale is an amillennialist.

not even restrict the judgment to the earth. This means that it sums up all the judgments on particular nations, as predicted in chapters 13–23, and goes beyond them.[3]

Isaiah 24 corresponds to the global judgments of Revelation (see Rev 1:7; 3:10). This universal judgment occurs because mankind has not obeyed his Creator (24:5). The punishment from God includes the removal of food and drink (v. 7) and rejoicing (v. 8). Desolation is in the cities (v. 12). These events correspond to the seal judgments of war, famine, and death discussed in Rev 6:3–8 which also detail global judgment to come. Yet while the vast majority of mankind is terrified and shaken from God's judgments, a righteous remnant exists throughout the world who "shout for joy" (14–16a). Then we are told that the earth itself is in turmoil. The earth is "split through" and "shaken violently" (v. 19). It "totters like a shack" (v. 20). Revelation 6:12–14 describes "a great earthquake" and "every mountain and island" being removed from their places. So what is predicted in Isaiah 24 coincides with what is described in Revelation, especially chapters 6–19. Isaiah 24 predicts wrath and judgment on the earth and its dwellers; Revelation 6–19 also describes God's wrath and judgment on the earth and its inhabitants. This sets the scene for Isa 24:21–23—a text that has relevance for a coming intermediate kingdom we know as the millennium.

Isaiah 24:21–23 and the Two-Phase Judgment

Isaiah speaks of a two-phase judgment in Isa 24:21–23:

> On that day the LORD will punish
> the host of heaven above
> and kings of the earth below.
> They will be gathered together
> like prisoners in a pit.
> They will be confined to a dungeon;
> after many days they will be punished.
> The moon will be put to shame
> and the sun disgraced,

---

[3] Geoffrey W. Grogan, "Isaiah," in *The Expositor's Bible Commentary*, vol. 6, ed. Frank E. Gaebelein (Grand Rapids: Zondervan, 1986), 6:151.

because the LORD of Hosts will reign as king
on Mount Zion in Jerusalem,
and He will display His glory
in the presence of His elders (Isa 24:21–23, HCSB).

In connection with the worldwide judgment of 24:1–20 this passage (Isa 24:21–23) shows there will be a *two-phase judgment of the enemies of God.* Before we look at this two-phase judgment, though, observe the links between what this passage describes and the events of Revelation 19 and 20:

Isa 24:21 mentions "kings of the earth" that are opposed to God.	**Rev 19:19** refers to "kings of the earth" who are opposed to God.
Isa 24:21 states that both the kings of the earth and the host of heaven will be incarcerated.	**Rev 19:21** tells of the defeat of the kings of the earth and **Rev 20:1 –3** tells of the binding of Satan.
Isa 24:22 mentions imprisonment in a dungeon/pit.	**Rev 20:1** mentions Satan's confinement in an "abyss" which is also called a "prison" in 20:7.
Isa 24:22 states that final punishment takes place "after many days."	**Rev 20:7–10** states that after a thousand years Satan is released for a short time and then sentenced to the lake of fire; **Rev 20:11–15** states that all unbelieving dead are sentenced to the lake of fire after the thousand years are completed.
Isa 24:23 states the Lord will reign as King.	**Rev 20:6** states that Christ will reign for a thousand years.

These parallels show a strong connection between Isaiah 24 and Revelation 19–20. Also, Isa 24:23 and its discussion of the moon and sun being diminished parallels Rev 21:23, which states that the New Jerusalem has no need of the sun or moon because of the glory of God through Jesus the Lamb.

Isaiah 24:22 is a backdrop for the millennial kingdom that John will discuss in Revelation 20.[4] Isaiah says that with God's judgments "the host of heaven" and the "kings of the earth" will be "gathered together" and "confined to a dungeon." And then he says their punishment will take place "after many days." The coming of the Lord and His kingdom means incarceration for these groups but their final judgment is not yet. This mention of "after many days" points to some intermediate situation—a situation explicitly discussed in Rev 20:1–6. As Blaising states, "The structure of the oracle in Isaiah 24–25 indicates some kind of intermediate situation between the coming of God in the Day of the Lord and the everlasting reign in which sin and death are done away completely."[5] Grogan notes that Isa 24:22 "harmonizes with a premillennial interpretation of Revelation."[6] So a connection with Revelation 20 exists:

> The many days of imprisonment between the coming of God in the Day of the Lord and the punishment after which the Lord reigns in glory greater than sun or moon bear a correspondence to the millennial period in Revelation 20, which also follows the coming of the Lord in the Day of the Lord.[7]

Other sections of Isaiah's Little Apocalypse also correspond to the events of Revelation 19–21:

Isa 25:6 says the Lord "will prepare a lavish banquet" for His people.	**Rev 19:9** says God's people "are invited to the marriage supper of the Lamb."
Isa 25:8 says the Lord "will swallow up death for all time."	**Rev 21:4** says "there will no longer be any death."
Isa 25: 8 states that the Lord God "will wipe tears away from all faces."	**Rev 21:4** states, "He will wipe away every tear from their eyes" and "there will no

---

[4] Beale and McDonough state, "Isaiah 24:21–22 is the basis for 20:2–3 . . . and finds its fulfillment there." "Revelation," in *Commentary on the New Testament Use of the Old Testament*, 1145.

[5] Craig A. Blaising, "Premillennialism," in *Three Views on the Millennium and Beyond*, 203.

[6] Grogan, "Isaiah," *EBC*, 6:155.

[7] Blaising, 203.

	longer be any mourning, or crying, or pain."
Isa 26:11 says "fire will devour your enemies."	**Rev 19:20; 20:9–10; and 20:14–15** mention God's enemies facing fiery judgment.
Isa 26:19 predicts bodily resurrection—"Your dead will live; their corpses will rise."	**Rev 20:4** says God's people "came to life."
Isa 27:1 predicts the punishment of the Leviathan serpent and the dragon who lives in the sea.	**Rev 20:2** states that Christ will incarcerate "the dragon, the serpent of old, who is the devil and Satan" and **Rev 20:7–10** state Satan's ultimate destiny is the lake of fire.

In sum, two points are worthy of note. First, the use of Isaiah 24–27 in Revelation shows that Revelation harmonizes with the message of Isaiah 24–27. What Isaiah predicted is also what Revelation foretells. Second, Isaiah 24–27 is a backdrop for the millennial kingdom discussed in Revelation 20. Isaiah 24:21–22 tells of a two-stage judgment separated by "many days" which in Revelation 20 will be described as a "thousand years."

Intermediate Kingdom Conditions Predicted in the Old Testament

Revelation 19:11–21:8 tells of an intermediate era between the present age and the Eternal State. But in addition to Revelation 20, *several Old Testament passages predict an era on this earth that is far better than the current age we live in but not yet as perfect as the coming Eternal State.* Thus, there is a necessity of an intermediate kingdom after the second coming of Jesus but before the Eternal State. As Wayne Grudem puts it:

> Several Old Testament passages seem to fit neither in the present age nor in the Eternal State. These passages indicate some future stage in the history of redemption which is far greater

than the present church age but which still does not see the removal of all sin and rebellion and death from the earth.[8]

Isaiah 65:20

One passage that points to an intermediate period is Isa 65:20. In discussing new earth conditions (65:17) this verse states:

> No more shall there be in it an infant that lives but a few days, or an old man who does not fill out his days, for the child shall die a hundred years old, and the sinner a hundred years old shall be accursed.

When this prophecy is fulfilled people will live so long that if they die at age 100 something must be wrong since people will live much longer than that. In fact, it will be assumed that a person dying at age 100 must be "accursed." So notice two important things here with Isa 65:20—an increased longevity of life and the presence of sin which brings curses and death.

Now we must ask the question, "When in history have these conditions described in Isa 65:20 occurred? Can it be during our present age?" The answer is clearly, no. We live in a day where people live between 70–80 years on average (see Ps 90:10). If a person dies today at age 100 we say he or she lived an exceptionally long life, not a short one. So, will Isa 65:20 be fulfilled in the coming Eternal State? The answer again must be, no. In the Eternal State there is no longer any sin, death, or curse (Rev 21:4; 22:3), so no one will die. Therefore, Isa 65:20 must be fulfilled in an era that is different from our current period yet distinct from the Eternal State. This means there must be an intermediate kingdom, or what we call a millennium. Compare the three eras:

---

[8] Wayne Grudem, *Systematic Theology: An Introduction to Biblical Doctrine* (Grand Rapids: Zondervan, 1994), 1127.

Present Age:	Life spans of 70–80 years
Millennial Kingdom:	Life spans well beyond 70–80 years but death still occurs.
Eternal State:	People live forever with no presence of sin, death, or curse.

This idea that Isaiah 65 is a reference to a future millennium is not recent. Christians of the second century viewed this passage as support for premillennialism. Martin Erdmann points out that Isa 65:20–25 formed "the scriptural basis, besides Revelation 20:1–10, on which Asiatic millennialism built its chiliastic doctrine."[9] This was also true for Justin Martyr. In reference to Isaiah 65 Justin said, "For Isaiah spoke thus concerning this period of a thousand years."[10] Erdmann points out that Justin's reference to Old Testament prophets "indicates his reliance on the Old Testament as the primary source of his chiliasm. He did not shy away from utilizing different passages from the Hebrew Bible to strengthen his argument in favor of a literal millennium."[11] Likewise, the author of the *Epistle of Barnabas* was a premillennialist, and according to Erdmann, "his chiliastic views are partially based on verses from the Old Testament."[12]

Zechariah 8

Zechariah 8 offers some descriptions of God's coming kingdom when Jesus returns. The chapter begins with God restoring Jerusalem. With "great wrath" and "jealousy" (8:2) the Lord returns to Zion and dwells in Jerusalem (8:3). The great city will have another name—"City of Truth" (8:3). This capital city of God's kingdom will be characterized by sweet peace and fellowship, as the Lord himself says:

---

[9] Martin Erdmann, *The Millennial Controversy in the Early Church* (Eugene, OR: Wipf and Stock, 2005), 118.

[10] Justin Martyr, *Dialogue with Trypho, The Ante-Nicene Fathers* 80, 1:239.

[11] Erdmann, 138.

[12] Ibid., 149.

Thus says the LORD of hosts, "Old men and old women will again sit in the streets of Jerusalem, each man with his staff in his hand because of age. And the streets of the city will be filled with boys and girls playing in its streets" (Zech 8:4–5).

When the Lord comes and reigns from Jerusalem, the elderly and young people will be talking and playing in the streets. It appears that age and age discrepancies still exist when the Lord's kingdom is established. Old men and women at this time will need the aid of a staff "because of age." They possess some weakness because of advanced years. This suggests the concept of an intermediate kingdom (or millennium), an era that is different from the present evil age but different also from the Eternal State in which all negative aspects of aging and death are removed. From Zechariah's time until now there has never been a time where the conditions of Zechariah 8 have happened. On the other hand, there will be no elderly who are weak in the final Eternal State, for all remnants of the curse have been removed (see Revelation 21 and 22). What Zechariah describes must take place in an initial phase of God's kingdom before the Eternal State begins. Such an intermediate state between the present age and the Eternal State is described in Revelation 20 where a thousand-year reign of Christ is emphasized.

Zechariah 14

Zechariah 14 also supports premillennialism. It describes kingdom conditions after the return of Jesus to earth. After a siege of Jerusalem verse 9 states that the "LORD will be King over all the earth" after His feet stand on the Mount of Olives (v. 4), but there will still be occasional disobedience and rebellion on the part of some nations. It is predicted that Egypt and other nations will be punished with drought when they do not obey the Lord as they should:

Then it will come about that any who are left of all the nations that went against Jerusalem will go up from year to year to worship the King, the LORD of hosts, and to celebrate the Feast of Booths. And it will be that whichever of the families of the earth does not go up to Jerusalem to worship the King, the LORD of hosts, there will be no rain on them. If the family of Egypt does not go up or enter, then no rain will fall on them; it will be the plague with which the LORD smites the nations who do not go up to celebrate the Feast of Booths. This will be the punishment of Egypt, and the punishment of all the nations who do not go up to celebrate the Feast of Booths (Zech 14:16–19).

Grudem states the issue well when he points out that the sin and punishment of the nations after Jesus returns does not fit the present age or the Eternal State:

> Here again the description does not fit the present age, for the Lord is King over all the earth in this situation. But it does not fit the Eternal State either, because of the disobedience and rebellion against the Lord that is clearly present.[13]

Thus, the events of Zechariah 14 best fit with a premillennial understanding of the kingdom. While people from all nations are being saved in the present age, the nations themselves do not obey our Lord (see Psalm 2). In fact, they persecute those who belong to God. In the millennial kingdom Jesus will rule the nations while He is physically present on earth. The nations will obey and submit to His rule, but as Zechariah 14 points out, whenever a nation does not act as it should there is punishment. On the other hand, in the Eternal State there will be absolutely no disobedience from the nations. The picture of the nations in the Eternal State is only positive. The kings of the nations bring their contributions to the New Jerusalem (see Rev 21:24) and the leaves of the tree of life are said to be for the healing of the nations (see Rev 22:2). To compare:

Present Age:	Jesus is in heaven and the nations do not yet submit to Jesus as King.
Millennial Kingdom:	Jesus rules the nations on earth and punishes those nations that do not act as they should.

---

[13] Grudem, *Systematic Theology*, 1129.

<u>Eternal State:</u>   The nations act exactly as they should with no need of punishment.

The idea of an earthly kingdom that comes after Jesus' return but before the Eternal State is consistent with several Old Testament passages. In the course of progressive revelation, Revelation 20 will reveal how long this intermediate kingdom will be ("a thousand years"), but it is not the first and only reference to such an era. When someone says, "You have only one passage, Revelation 20, which allegedly teaches a millennium," the answer is, "That's not true. Revelation 20 tells us how long Christ's intermediate earthly kingdom will be—one thousand years—but other passages teach the idea of an intermediate kingdom." Premillennialism, therefore, is a doctrine found in both testaments.

5

THE COMING KINGDOM REIGN ON EARTH

A key component of premillennialism is that Jesus' millennial kingdom is both future and earthly. Several passages in the New Testament affirm this understanding. This contrasts with other millennial views which see the millennial kingdom as present and spiritual in nature.

Revelation 5:10 and the Coming Reign

About sixty years into the church age (ca. A.D. 90), the apostle John received visions concerning events to come. According to Revelation 5, he was allowed to see a scene in heaven where twenty-four elders sang a new song:

"You have made them to be a kingdom and priests to our God; and they will reign upon the earth" (Rev 5:10).

The ones Jesus purchased with His blood (5:9) are "a kingdom." They are positionally related to the kingdom because they know King Jesus. Yet this positional status will lead to an actual kingdom reign—"and they will reign upon the earth." Being positionally related to the kingdom results eventually in a coming kingdom reign.

Three points are significant for understanding Messiah's kingdom from Rev 5:10. First, the saints of God are destined to reign with Christ. There is a close connection between the reign of the Messiah and the reign of the saints. When Jesus reigns, the saints will also reign. Other passages present the reign of the saints as future. In 1 Cor 4:8 Paul made a brief statement to the Corinthians who were acting as if they were already reigning. He said, "You are already filled, you have already become rich, you have become kings without us; and indeed, I wish that you had become kings so that we also might reign with you." The Corinthians were acting like they had arrived, that they were reigning in God's kingdom already. But Paul sarcastically mocks their attitude. He plays along and says that they have become "filled" and "rich." "You have become kings without us," he declared. Paul then switches back to reality by telling them, "I wish that you had become kings so that we also might reign with you." Contrary to the way the Corinthians were acting, Paul says that they were not reigning. It would be nice if they were reigning because Paul would like to be reigning too. But that was not reality yet.

Second, Rev 5:10 indicates that this reign is future—"they *will* reign." The present age is an era of persecution and trial from Satan and his servants. That is why Jesus offers future rewards to the seven churches of Asia Minor (see Revelation 2–3). But a day is coming when the tables will be turned and those who are persecuted by the world will reign.

Third, this coming reign of the saints is "upon the earth." This shows that the kingdom of Christ is an earthly reign. This is not a reign that only exists in heaven or in the church or in the hearts of men. It is an earthly kingdom. The promise that the saints will reign upon the earth finds its culmination with Rev 20:4 when the saints will sit on thrones and judgment is given to them. A close connection exists between Rev 5:10 and Rev 20:4. The former is the promise of a coming reign, the latter describes the inauguration of that reign.

The Future Rule of Messiah and the Saints

Several other passages place the reign of Jesus and the saints in the future. Notice the future tense in the following:

- 1 Cor 6:2: Or do you not know that the saints will judge the world?

- 1 Cor 6:3: Do you not know that we will judge angels?

- 2 Tim 2:12a: If we endure, we will also reign with Him.

- Rev 2:26–27: He who overcomes, and he who keeps My deeds until the end, TO HIM I WILL GIVE AUTHORITY OVER

THE NATIONS; <u>AND HE SHALL RULE THEM</u> WITH A ROD OF
IRON, AS THE VESSELS OF THE POTTER ARE BROKEN TO
PIECES, as I also have received authority from My Father;

- Rev 12:5: And she gave birth to a son, a male child, <u>who is
to rule all the nations</u> with a rod of iron; and her child was
caught up to God and to His throne.

- Rev 19:15: From His mouth comes a sharp sword, so that
with it He may strike down the nations, and <u>He will rule
them</u> with a rod of iron; and He treads the wine press of the
fierce wrath of God, the Almighty.

First Corinthians 6:2–3 states the Christians "will" judge the
world and angels. This truth should influence their judgment in the
present. Second Timothy 2:12 indicates that enduring for Jesus now
will lead to a "reign" with Jesus. Reigning is not occurring now but
will be the case later. The three passages in Revelation refer back to
Psalm 2, where it is revealed that God's King and Son will rule the
nations with a rod of iron. Revelation 12:5 and 19:15 reiterate this
truth that Jesus the Messiah will rule the nations with a rod of iron.
Revelation 2:26–27 says Jesus will share His rule with those who
know Him and overcome the world in this age.

What is significant about these references is they place Jesus'
rule and the reign of the saints over the nations in the future. With
Rev 2:26–27 the promise of ruling the nations is offered as a future
reward to overcomers in the church. Ruling the nations is not their
current experience. Also, Jesus tells the church of Thyatira, "hold
fast until I come" (2:25). If they "hold fast" until the coming of Jesus,
they will be rewarded with ruling functions in the kingdom of Christ.
In sum, ruling the nations is a reward that Jesus brings to His own
when He comes.

The Rev 19:15 passage is also important because the statement
that Jesus will "strike down the nations" and "rule them with a rod
of iron" comes within the context of Jesus' second coming, which is
the subject of Rev 19:11–21. It is Jesus' second coming that leads to
the ruling of the nations with a rod of iron. Revelation 1:5 tells us
that Jesus is "the ruler of the kings of the earth." Yet it is with His
second coming that He actually rules the nations.

The Coming Reign of Messiah from David's Throne at the Second Coming

Another evidence for premillennialism is found with Matt 19:28 and 25:31, where Jesus says He will assume His glorious Davidic throne at the time of His second coming. This is very significant. Jesus explicitly ties His Davidic throne reign with His second coming to earth and not before. This shows that Jesus' kingdom is future from our standpoint. *The kingdom comes when Jesus comes again.* This truth makes amillennialism and postmillennialism impossible since these positions assert that Jesus is now reigning from the Davidic throne in His millennial kingdom in this age.

The throne of David, which finds is roots in the Davidic Covenant promises of 2 Samuel 7, is linked with Jesus who is the ultimate Son of David. When the angel, Gabriel, appeared to Mary, he stated the following concerning her coming Son:

> "He will be great and will be called the Son of the Most High; and the Lord God will give Him the throne of His father David; and He will reign over the house of Jacob forever, and His kingdom will have no end."

Gabriel made clear that Jesus was coming so He could be given the throne of David and reign over Israel. With Matt 25:31 Jesus addresses when He will assume that throne:

> "But when the Son of Man comes in His glory, and all the angels with Him, then He will sit on His glorious throne."

The word for "then" (*tote*) is an adverb of time and means "at that time." The term for "will sit" is *kathisei* and is in the future tense. The Davidic throne, therefore, is linked with two things: (1) the Son of Man coming in glory and (2) all the angels coming with Him. When those two events occur the Son of Man will then "sit upon His glorious throne." *Therefore, sitting upon the glorious Davidic throne by Jesus occurs at the time of His coming in glory with His angels.*

This is the strongest possible evidence concerning the timing of Jesus' kingdom. Jesus explicitly states, in a prophetic context, when He will assume the Davidic throne. It is when He comes in glory with the angels. This event is future from our standpoint. Since

Jesus has not returned in glory yet with all of His angels, we can know that He has not yet assumed the Davidic throne. A similar statement by Jesus is found in Matt 19:28 which also links Jesus' throne with other future events:

> And Jesus said to them, "Truly I say to you, that you who have followed Me, in the regeneration <u>when the Son of Man will sit on His glorious throne, you also shall sit upon twelve thrones, judging the twelve tribes of Israel.</u>"

Again we see Jesus referring to sitting upon "His glorious throne" in a future context. Here, Jesus is talking about future rewards for His disciples. Importantly, He ties it with an event called "the regeneration." Most scholars believe Jesus is speaking of the renewal of the cosmos, the glorification for creation (see Rom 8:19–23). The word "regeneration" is the Greek term *palingenesia* which means "regeneration," "renewal," or "genesis again." J. I. Packer says, "it denotes the eschatological 'restoration of all things' (Acts 3:21) under the Messiah for which Israel was waiting."[1] This renewal must be future since we have not seen a glorification of the creation yet.

When this cosmic renewal occurs, two other things come with it: (1) the Son of Man sitting on His glorious throne; and (2) the apostles judging/ruling the twelve tribes of Israel. Both refer to kingdom and ruling functions. Jesus' sitting on the glorious throne of David has not occurred yet, but it will occur in the future at the time of the renewal of the world and the apostles ruling over a restored national Israel. So with Matt 19:28 Jesus tells us His Davidic kingdom throne reign will occur with other glorious future events. He does not say that His second coming brings an end or culmination of His kingdom reign. This strongly supports premillennialism while making amillennialism and postmillennialism impossible. If Jesus' Davidic and mediatorial reign begins with the second coming this means Jesus' kingdom must be future and is not in operation in this age. As 1 Cor 15:24–28 reveals, Jesus must reign over His enemies successfully before He hands the kingdom over to the Father. According to Jesus in Matt 19:28 and 25:31, this Davidic reign begins at His second coming.

---

[1] J. I. Packer, "Regeneration," in *Evangelical Dictionary of Theology*, ed. Walter A. Elwell (Grand Rapids: Baker Book House, 1984), 925.

6

THE MILLENNIUM AND REVELATION 19–20

The case for a future earthly kingdom of Christ has been established by several passages in both testaments. Now our attention shifts to Revelation 19–20. This passage explicitly teaches a future intermediate kingdom of a thousand years:

> Then I saw an angel coming down from heaven, holding the key of the abyss and a great chain in his hand. And he laid hold of the dragon, the serpent of old, who is the devil and Satan, and bound him for a thousand years; and he threw him into the abyss, and shut it and sealed it over him, so that he would not deceive the nations any longer, until the thousand years were completed; after these things he must be released for a short time. Then I saw thrones, and they sat on them, and judgment was given to them. And I saw the souls of those who had been beheaded because of their testimony of Jesus and because of the word of God, and those who had not worshiped the beast or his image, and had not received the mark on their forehead and on their hand; and they came to life and reigned with Christ for a thousand years. The rest of the dead did not come to life until the thousand years were completed. This is the first resurrection. Blessed and holy is the one who has a part in the first resurrection; over these the second death has no power, but they will be priests of God and of Christ and will reign with Him for a thousand years. When the thousand years are completed, Satan will be released from his prison, and will come out to deceive the nations which are in the four corners of the earth,

Gog and Magog, to gather them together for the war; the number of them is like the sand of the seashore. And they came up on the broad plain of the earth and surrounded the camp of the saints and the beloved city, and fire came down from heaven and devoured them. And the devil who deceived them was thrown into the lake of fire and brimstone, where the beast and the false prophet are also; and they will be tormented day and night forever and ever (Rev 20:1-10).

This section can be summarized as follows:

- Satan will be bound and thrown into a prison where all his activities are completely ceased for a thousand years (1–3).
- Positions of kingdom authority are granted to previously martyred saints (4).
- These martyrs who were slain for the testimony of Jesus are resurrected and reign with Christ for a thousand years (4).
- Another group, "the rest of the dead," come to life one thousand years later (5).
- Those who are part of the first resurrection are priests of God and Christ and will reign with Him for a thousand years (6).
- At the end of the thousand years Satan is released and leads a rebellion that is immediately defeated with fire from heaven (7–10).

That this millennium is both earthly and future can be understood from several aspects. But before doing so, the genre of the book of Revelation must be understood.

Genre of Revelation: Prophecy

The book of Revelation describes what John experienced and saw via divine revelation:

The Revelation of Jesus Christ, which God gave Him to show to His bond-servants, the things which must soon take place; and He sent and communicated it by His angel to His bondservant John, who testified to the word of God and to the testimony of Jesus Christ, even to all that he saw (Rev 1:1–2).

What John receives is a "revelation" (*apokalupsis*) of Jesus Christ. Jesus Christ is pictured as a revealer of information that God wanted for His servants.[1] Jesus "communicated" or "signified" this revelation by an angel to John.[2] Jesus then refers to the prophetic nature of this revelation to be given:

> Blessed is he who reads and those who hear the words of the prophecy, and heed the things which are written in it (Rev 1:3a).

The nature of this revelation is "prophecy." In continuity with the prophets of the Old Testament, John received divinely inspired revelation that is prophetic in nature. This is a case where the genre of the book of Revelation is explicitly stated. The genre is *prophecy*. Often much is made of the alleged "apocalyptic" nature of Revelation in which John supposedly wrote in the style of non-inspired Jewish apocalyptic writers of his era. Such discussion is complicated since there is considerable disagreement concerning how to define "apocalyptic genre." It is also complicated by the fact that Revelation has elements that do not fit with the traditional understanding of "apocalyptic." For instance, with apocalyptic literature the real author is not known, but in the case of Revelation we know its author—John. Also, Revelation has an epistolary section to it (chaps. 2–3), something other apocalyptic literature writings do not have.

So is there no relation between Revelation and apocalyptic genre? The answer depends on what one means by apocalyptic. If one identifies apocalyptic as divine revelation about the future in the

---

[1] There is some issue as to whether Jesus is the One being revealed or the One who is doing the revealing. The latter view is more likely. As Thomas states, "it refers to data that Jesus Christ was inspired by God to reveal to His servants." Robert L. Thomas, *Revelation 1–7: An Exegetical Commentary* (Chicago: Moody, 1992), 52.

[2] Some claim that the word "signify" (*semaino*) is an indicator that the contents of the revelation are to be understood non-literally or symbolically. But this is reading too much into the term. The meaning here is that Jesus is going to "show," "announce" or "declare" the contents of the revelation without indicating that there are cryptic meanings behind the terms used.

form of visions and symbols given to a prophet under divine inspiration, then, yes, the book of Revelation is apocalyptic. So too were prophetic books such as Daniel, Ezekiel, and Zechariah. But if one views John as mimicking the genre of other Jewish apocalyptic writers of his day who were not inspired then there are some problems.[3] John was writing under inspiration from God. The contents of his writings were not his own inventions but stemmed from actual revelations from God. And unlike other apocalyptic writers of his era, John did not sit down to intentionally write cryptic messages. He did not say to himself, "I need to give my people encouragement in difficult times so I am going to use cryptic symbols to encourage them." If we take John at His word, he is writing down what God revealed to him via an angel of God. And unlike some others, he is doing so under inspiration. For those who accept the supernatural nature of the Bible this should be no surprise. For John to see the resurrected Jesus who gives spectacular, timeless visions with vivid symbols representing literal truths is consistent with a revealing God. Other sections of Revelation confirm the prophetic nature of the book of Revelation:

> Blessed is he who heeds the words of the prophecy of this book (Rev 22:7).

> And he said to me, "Do not seal up the words of the prophecy of this book, for the time is near" (Rev 22:10).

> "I testify to everyone who hears the words of the prophecy of this book . . ." (Rev 22:18a).

> "and if anyone takes away from the words of the book of this prophecy . . ." (Rev 22:19a).

---

[3] Ladd observes that "apocalyptic writings appeared between 200 B.C. and A.D. 100, which purported to bring revelations from God explaining the reason for the prevalence of evil, disclosing heavenly secrets, and promising the imminent coming of His kingdom and the salvation of the afflicted." George E. Ladd, "Apocalyptic," in *The New Bible Dictionary*, ed. by J. D. Douglas (Grand Rapids: William B. Eerdmans Publishing Company, 1962), 1:43. First Enoch, Jubilees, the Assumption of Moses, 4 Ezra, 2 Esdras, the Apocalypse of Baruch, and the Testaments of the Twelve Patriarchs were written during this time.

So we do not have to guess what kind of literature Revelation is. The book of Revelation, including its discussion of the millennium in Rev 20:1–6, is prophecy. Its intent is to give prophetic information about the future. Many of the details of this prophecy will be given in the form of symbols, but behind these symbols are literal truths that are usually explained in the book of Revelation itself or grasped from other Scripture passages where these symbols are used (e.g., Rev 12:1-6 with Gen 37:9-11).

Literary Structure

Where do the events of Revelation 20 fit within the overall structure of Revelation? Below is a listing of the major sections of Revelation:

Prologue	1:1–1:8
Letters to Seven Churches	1:9–3:22
Heavenly Court and Its Judgment	4:1–11:19
Prophetic/Apocalyptic Narrative	12:1–16:21
Fall of Babylon	17:1–19:10
Prophetic/Apocalyptic Narrative	19:11–21:8
New Jerusalem Established	21:9–22:9
Epilogue	22:10–22:21

John's discussion of the millennium comes within the section of 19:11–21:8, a section that describes the return of Jesus and events after His return. Here John uses the expression *kai eidon* eight times (19:11, 17, 19; 20:1, 4, 11, 12; 21:1). *Kai eidon* can be translated "and I saw" or "then I saw." This expression can refer to chronological progression which seems to be the case here. As Robert Mounce observed, "It should be noted that the recurring 'and I saw' of 19:11, 17, 19; 20:1, 4, 12; and 21:1 appears to establish a sequence of visions which carries through from the appearance of the Rider on the white horse (19:11) to the establishment of the new heaven and new earth (21:1ff)."[4]

As the events within 19:11–21:8 unfold, John tells of several things he saw in succession, one after the other:

---

[4] Robert H. Mounce, *The Book of Revelation*, NICNT (Grand Rapids: Eerdmans, 1977), 352.

19:11–16: John saw ("And I saw") the return of Christ with the armies of heaven to strike down Christ's enemies and rule the nations.

19:17–18: Then John saw ("Then I saw") an angel in heaven calling to the birds to eat the flesh of the enemies of Christ.

19:19–21 Then John saw ("And I saw") the beast and the armies of the earth wage war against the returning Christ; the beast and the false prophet are seized and thrown into the lake of fire and the rest of the enemies are slain.

20:1–3: Then John saw ("Then I saw") an angel coming from heaven with a great chain to bind Satan and throw him into the pit where his evil activities are totally ceased.

20:4–10: Then John saw ("Then I saw") thrones established, the resurrection of the martyrs and their reigning with Christ for a thousand years, and the rest of the dead coming to life after the thousand years are completed. After the thousand-year period is over, Satan is released from his prison and leads a rebellion of nations against God's people and the holy city. Satan is defeated and thrown into the lake of fire.

20:11: Then John saw ("Then I saw") a great white throne established that could not be escaped.

20:12–15: Then John saw ("And I saw") the great and the small judged, with those whose names were not found in the book of life being cast into the lake of fire; death and Hades were thrown into the lake of fire.

21:1–8: Then John saw ("Then I saw") a new heaven and a new earth and the coming of the New Jerusalem.

The main point here is that in Rev 19:11–21:8, John describes the second coming of Jesus and the events that follow it. This includes the thousand-year reign of Christ of Rev 20:1–10. The events of Rev 20:1–10 follow the second coming of Jesus described in Rev 19:11ff. There is sequential progression, not recapitulation in this section.

This understanding is a logical conclusion based on a section that is describing a chronological progression of events. As Craig Blaising observes, "It is noteworthy . . . that when the issue of theological-historical significance is suspended and the question is strictly literary, there is general agreement that the events in the visions of 19:11–21:8 are correlative with or consequent to the Parousia of 19:11."[5]

Six of the eight visions that start with "and/then I saw" in 19:11–21:8 are commonly viewed as happening at the time of or after the events of the *parousia* as described in 19:11. The only two debated ones are 20:1–3 and 4–7, which describe the binding of Satan and the reign of the saints. Amillennialists and postmillennialists place these sections between the two comings of Jesus. But is it not simpler to understand all eight sections as describing events after the coming of Jesus? It seems arbitrary to claim six of these are post-*parousia*, but two of them are not. Blaising is correct that, "The presumption is in favor of viewing the remaining two visions [found in 20:1–6] in a similar manner."[6] Mounce is also accurate that "The interpretation that discovers recapitulation for the segment 20:1–6 must at least bear the burden of proof."[7]

Also, the chronological understanding based on a proper understanding of the literary context makes most sense of what is described in Revelation 19 and 20. This section tells of the defeat of the false trinity that is opposed to God—Satan, the beast, and the false prophet. As the beast and the false prophet are defeated by the returning Christ in 19:19–21, the attention turns to what will happen to Satan who is the power behind the beast and the false prophet? A chronological progression view understands that at Christ's return Satan will be dealt with too. Off the heels of the defeat of the beast and the false prophet, Rev 20:1–3 finds Satan incarcerated and put in a prison. All three enemies are defeated with the return of King Jesus.

But if one insists that Revelation 19 is about the second coming of Jesus, yet Rev 20:1 takes the reader back to the beginning of the church age, then there is a disconnect concerning when God deals

---

[5] Craig A. Blaising, "Premillennialism," in *Three Views on the Millennium and Beyond*, ed. Darrell L. Bock (Grand Rapids: Zondervan, 1999), 213.

[6] Ibid., 216.

[7] Mounce, 352.

with His ultimate enemies. In this odd scenario, Satan is bound at the beginning of the church age, but the beast and the false prophet who are empowered by Satan are not defeated until the second coming of Jesus. It seems better to view all three members of the false trinity dealt with at the same time. Thus, the best understanding is that Christ appears from heaven (19:11–19), He destroys His enemies, including the beast and the false prophet (19:20–21), and then He deals with the third member of the false trinity, Satan, by binding him and casting him into the abyss (20:1–3). Blomberg summarizes this well:

> In the process, we are told about the fate of two of the three members of the so-called satanic trinity introduced in 12:1–13:18. The beast and the false prophet, parodies of Jesus and the Holy Spirit, are captured and thrown alive into the lake of fire (19:20). Readers expect to hear next about the fate of the ringleader of the three, Satan himself, the one who wanted to usurp the place of God the Father, and they are not disappointed. Revelation 20:1 continues seamlessly, describing Satan's confinement to the abyss until the very end of the millennium. The rest of the chapter follows equally inexorably from there on.[8]

Sequence of events in this section makes the most sense. George Ladd was correct when he declared, "There is absolutely no hint of any recapitulation in chapter 20."[9] And as Blomberg has aptly stated, "No matter how many flashbacks or disruptions of chronological sequence one might want to argue for elsewhere in Revelation, it makes absolutely no sense to put one in between Revelation 19 and 20 as both amillennialists and postmillennialists must do."[10]

---

[8] Craig L. Blomberg, "The Posttribulationism of the New Testament," in *A Case for Historic Premillennialism: An Alternative to 'Left Behind' Eschatology*, eds., Craig L. Blomberg and Sung Wook Chung (Grand Rapids: Baker, 2009), 68.

[9] George Eldon Ladd, "An Historical Premillennial Response," in *The Meaning of the Millennium: Four Views*, ed. Robert G. Clouse (Downers Grove: Inter Varsity, 1977), 190.

[10] Blomberg, 67.

The Binding of Satan (Rev 20:1–3)

Another reason for holding to a future and earthly understanding of the millennium of Revelation 20 is the nature of the binding of Satan described in Rev 20:1–3. This passage describes an incarceration of Satan which results in a complete cessation of his activities:

> Then I saw an angel coming down from heaven, holding the key of the abyss and a great chain in his hand. And he laid hold of the dragon, the serpent of old, who is the devil and Satan, and bound him for a thousand years; and he threw him into the abyss, and shut it and sealed it over him, so that he would not deceive the nations any longer, until the thousand years were completed; after these things he must be released for a short time.

The language here is powerful. Note several truths concerning the fate of Satan:

1. Satan is "bound."
2. Satan is thrown into the abyss.
3. The abyss that Satan is placed into is "shut" and "sealed" over him.

Much attention has focused on whether the activities of Satan are merely curtailed or ceased altogether. Amillennialists and postmillennialists argue for a hindering of Satan's activities while premillennialists claim both Satan and his doings are halted altogether. But before one even considers the activities of Satan, one must recognize what is happening to Satan himself, as a personal being. Satan is incarcerated and confined in a real place, a place called "the abyss" which functions as a prison. *More than a specific function of Satan (i.e. deceiving nations) is hindered; Satan himself is absolutely confined to a place that results in a complete cessation of all that he does.*

Satan is imprisoned. He used to inflict his evil ways on the earth but now he is no longer able to do so because his presence is transferred to the abyss. In Rev 9:1–3 the "bottomless pit" or "abyss" was a place where locust-like beings were confined. But their release from the abyss means they were free to do their damaging activities "upon the earth" (9:3). While they were in the abyss they were not free to do anything on the earth. Also, with the account of the demoniac in Luke 8, many demons pleaded with Jesus so they would not be sent to the "abyss" (8:31). They were afraid of being removed from having any presence or influence on earth, and not just a curtailing of their activities. So the abyss is a real spirit prison that houses demonic beings.

Since Satan has been removed from the earth to imprisonment in the abyss, conclusions can be made concerning what this means for his activities. Since Satan as a personal being is confined to the abyss, his major activity—deceiving the nations—ceased as well. But the main reason Satan is no longer able to deceive the nations is because he is in prison with no access to the earth. *Imprisonment of a person means a cessation of that person's works.* To use an example, if a police officer captures a serial killer who terrorized a city and puts him in prison we could say, "This wicked person has been jailed so that he cannot continue with his murdering ways." Such a statement does not mean only this person's murdering activities are curtailed. Nor does it mean that he is free to rape and rob. That would be absurd. His incarceration as a person means his wicked ways have totally stopped. Likewise, the binding of Satan means for the first time in human history mankind will not have to deal with Satan's deceptive tactics. Mounce is correct when he states: "The elaborate measures taken to insure his [Satan's] custody are most easily understood as implying the complete cessation of his influence on earth (rather than a curbing of his activities)."[11]

This truth that Satan is incarcerated during the millennium is not compatible amillennialism and postmillennialism. Both positions assert that the millennium is present during this present age and that Satan is active. Supposedly, his limitation is that he is not able to stop the gospel from going to the nations. This view, though, has problems. The Scripture indicates that Satan's ability to deceive is alive and well in this present age:

> 2 Cor 4:4: "And even if our gospel is veiled, it is veiled to those who are perishing, in whose case the god of this world has blinded the minds of the unbelieving so that they might not see

---

[11] Mounce, 353.

the light of the gospel of the glory of Christ, who is the image of God."

1 Pet 5:8: "Be of sober spirit, be on the alert. Your adversary, the devil, prowls around like a roaring lion, seeking someone to devour."

1 John 5:19: "the whole world lies in the power of the evil one."

These passages, written by three different apostles after the death, resurrection, and ascension of Jesus, make clear that Satan is still actively involved in worldwide deception. Plus, Revelation itself explicitly states that before Jesus returns, Satan is actively deceiving the nations with much success. Revelation 12:9 declares:

> And the great dragon was thrown down, the serpent of old who is called the devil and Satan, who deceives the whole world; he was thrown down to the earth, and his angels were thrown down with him.

The sphere of Satan's deception before Jesus returns is "the whole world." This worldwide deception over the nations is again discussed in Rev 13:2, 7–8:

> And the dragon [Satan] gave him [the Beast] his power and his throne and great authority . . . . It was also given to him [the Beast] to make war with the saints and to overcome them, and authority over every tribe and people and tongue and nation was given to him. All who dwell on the earth will worship him.

Satan is the energizing power behind the beast who has authority over "every tribe and people and tongue and nation." Thus, in the period between the two comings of Jesus, Satan is characterized by deceiving every people group. This is why the binding of Satan described in Rev 20:1–3 is so dramatic and historic. Before Jesus comes again Satan's deceptive power over the nations is strong but in one moment his ability to deceive the nations will end. This passage contradicts any theology that says Satan's ability to deceive the nations is bound today. As Wayne Grudem points out, "It seems more appropriate to say that Satan is *now* still deceiving the nations, but at the beginning of the millennium this deceptive influence will be removed."[12]

Those who assert that the binding of Satan is taking place in this present age between the two comings of Jesus often link the events of Rev 20:1–3 with Jesus' victory over Satan at the cross. Of course, Jesus was victorious over Satan at the cross. Yet the cosmic battle between God and Satan includes a series of battles that eventually culminate in Satan's imprisonment in the lake of fire (see Rev 20:10). Just as a major war between nations involves many battles, so too, the battle between God and Satan involves several battles. God's victory over Satan involves several events:

1. Satan judged and cast down from heaven before the fall of man (Isa 14:12–15; Ezek 28:11–19).

2. Jesus' demonstrations of power over Satan's realm through his casting out of demons (Matt 12:28).

3. Jesus' victory over Satan at the cross (Col 2:15).

4. Satan thrown from heaven to the earth for a short time shortly before the return of Jesus (Rev 12:7-9).

5. Satan bound in the pit for one thousand years at the return of Jesus (Rev 20:1–3).

6. Satan sent to the lake of fire forever after the thousand-year reign of Jesus (Rev 20:7–10).

These are separate but interrelated events in the cosmic war. But the binding of Satan described in Rev 20:1–3 occurs after Jesus returns to earth at His second coming, not before.

Two Physical Resurrections (Rev 20:4–5)

Another evidence for a future understanding of the millennium is found in the two resurrections of Rev 20:4–5. *The fulfillment of these*

---

[12] Wayne Grudem, *Systematic Theology: An Introduction to Biblical Doctrine* (Grand Rapids: Zondervan, 1994), 1118.

two resurrections must be future from our standpoint in history; this shows that the millennium is future as well.

In verse 4, John says that "the souls of those who had been beheaded because of their testimony of Jesus . . . came to life and reigned with Christ for a thousand years." This group of souls who were beheaded is the same group of martyrs who came out of the great tribulation described in Revelation 6. Thus, there is a connection between the martyrs of Revelation 6 and the martyrs who will be resurrected in Revelation 20.

Revelation 6:9–11 describes the fifth seal which is the martyrdom of God's people who were slain because of their commitment to the Word of God and their testimony for Jesus (see Rev 6:9). This solemn passage tells of the condition of the souls of martyred saints. Their state is not that of "reigning." Instead, it is one of crying to the Lord for the avenging of their lives. These saints were killed for their testimony on the earth. And now their souls are in heaven and they are crying out, "How long, O Lord, holy and true, will You refrain from judging and avenging our blood on those who dwell on the earth?" (6:10). Verse 11 then states that these martyrs were clothed in white and told to "rest for a little while longer" until the full number of martyred saints was completed. While certainly at rest, these saints are not involved in a kingdom reign; instead, they are eagerly calling on the Lord to deal with their enemies who killed them. The response given to them is to wait for a while.

The frustration of these saints comes to an end, though, with the events of Revelation 19 and 20. Revelation 5:10 promised a coming day when the saints would reign upon the earth: "You have made them to be a kingdom and priests to our God; and they will reign upon the earth." Now this expectation is coming true. The enemies of Jesus receive judgment. And with the Lord's return, His saints will reign with Him. This is the picture presented in Rev 20:4–6.

Revelation 19:11–21 tells of the return of Jesus and the vanquishing of His enemies. Revelation 20:1–3 details the complete cessation of the activities of Satan. Then verse 4 declares that thrones are established, indicating a kingdom reign. Then the martyred saints "came to life and reigned with Christ for a thousand years." These are the same people who lost their physical lives in Rev 6:9–11. But now they come to life. The term for "came to life" is *ezēsan*, a word used of Jesus' bodily resurrection in Rev 2:8. Here Jesus referred to himself as, "The first and the last, who was dead, and has come to life (*ezēsan*)." The coming to life that Jesus referred to is not spiritual salvation, since Jesus did not need to be saved. Instead, His was a physical resurrection, a physical coming to life. The Jesus who was killed physically is the same Jesus who was raised physically from the dead. Likewise, these martyrs for the cause of Jesus who had physically died (Rev 6:9–11) are now physically made alive (Rev 20:4).

Verse 5 then states, "The rest of the dead did not come to life until the thousand years were completed." We are introduced now to another group called "the rest of the dead." This is a different group than the one mentioned in verse 4. It is said of this second group that they did not "come to life" until the thousand years were over.

Again, the term for "come to life," *ezēsan*, is used. Since *ezēsan* referred to physical resurrection in verse 4, it is highly likely if not certain that *ezēsan* refers to physical resurrection in verse 5. Such a conclusion is based on strong contextual and historical/grammatical considerations, for it is likely that the term *ezēsan* would be used similarly in such close proximity. Thus, a thousand years after the first group was physically resurrected this second group experiences physical resurrection. For the second group, though, this physical resurrection is unto eternal judgment. Verse 6 then states, "Blessed and holy is the one who has a part in the first resurrection; over these the second death has no power, but they will be priests of God and of Christ and will reign with Him for a thousand years." Those who experience the first resurrection will not experience what is called "the second death." But the people who are part of the second resurrection after the thousand years are affected by "the second death." This second death is linked with the lake of fire (20:14) that comes as a result of the great white throne judgment of Rev 20:11–15.

All of this points to a thousand-year period that separates the first physical resurrection of believers from the second resurrection of unbelievers to judgment. Amillennialists and postmillennialists admit that the second resurrection of 20:5 is a physical resurrection. But they claim that the first reference to *ezēsan* ("came to life") is a spiritual resurrection, akin to regeneration or spiritual birth at salvation. The problem with this understanding is evident. That the term, *ezēsan*, could be used in two different senses—spiritual resurrection and then physical resurrection—in such close proximity seems most improbable if not impossible. No evidence exists that the two terms should be understood in different ways. This inconsistent understanding of the two uses *egēsan* in such close proximity is a major problem for the non-premillennial views.

Also, the martyrs who gave their lives for the cause of Christ are not in need of spiritual resurrection. They are already saved. That is why they gave their lives for Jesus in the first place. But martyrs who have lost their physical lives to God's enemies are in need of a physical resurrection, and this is what Rev 20:4 promises. The first "came to life" in in 20:4, therefore, must refer to physical resurrection.

Amillennialists and postmillennialists admit that the second resurrection of Rev 20:5 cannot be a spiritual resurrection, for if it were, this would be teaching universalism, the view that all people will be saved. So 20:5 must be a physical resurrection from the dead. But if the second resurrection is a physical resurrection, what contextual reasons are there for claiming that the first resurrection of 20:4 is spiritual as non-premillennialists affirm? The claim that the resurrection of verse 4 is spiritual but the resurrection of verse 5 is physical is unsustainable.

Some appeal to John 5:19–28 in which Jesus speaks of both spiritual life now for believers and physical resurrection for believers and unbelievers in the future. They want to project this passage onto Rev 20:4–5 to affirm that the first "came to life" statement is about spiritual resurrection while the second is about physical resurrection. But the context of Rev 20:4 is specifically speaking about martyrs who gave their physical lives for Jesus (see Rev 6:9–11). These are not unbelievers who become spiritually alive, they are believers who come alive with physical resurrection. The situation in John 5:28–29 is different from what John is addressing in Rev 20:4–5. We cannot take the context of one passage and impose it on another passage to try and make it fit with our theology. The immediate context of Revelation 20 indicates two physical resurrections separated by a thousand years.

From another angle, some have asserted that when it comes to the two resurrections in Rev 20:4–5, it is not *chronology* that is in view but the *quality* of the resurrections. Thus, the first resurrection is a kind of resurrection focused on spiritual salvation, while the second resurrection concerns physical resurrection. Yet such a view does injustice to the immediate context which is time-oriented. The eight "and I saw" (*kai eidon*) markers in Rev 19:11–21:8 indicate chronology. And even more striking is that the second resurrection is said to follow the first resurrection by a "thousand years," showing that time is in view. When "years" are referred to, this involves time. So to deemphasize chronology here is a violation of the context since time is part of the context.

In sum, the best interpretation is that the martyrs who were killed for the sake of Jesus receive a physical resurrection, while a thousand years later there will be a physical resurrection to damnation for unbelievers. All of this argues for a future millennium. *If the two resurrections of Rev 20:4–5 are physical resurrections, then the millennium of Revelation 20 must be future, following the second coming of Jesus in Revelation 19. Since physical resurrection of the saints has not occurred in history, such a resurrection must be a future event and cannot be something fulfilled in this inter-advent age.* So Rev 20:4–5 is powerful evidence for an intermediate age, a millennium, after the second coming of Jesus but before the final Eternal State.

7

WHY PREMILLENNIALISM MUST BE TRUE

The main reason to affirm premillennialism is because the Bible explicitly teaches it. In one sense that's the main issue. But are there reasons for such a kingdom? Is there a rationale for premillennialism? Can we understand why a premillennial kingdom is necessary and so important to God's purposes? I think we can. Premillennialism fits well with the overall storyline of the Bible and explains what the restoration of all things (Acts 3:21) means and looks like. There are at least four reasons why there must be a premillennial kingdom of Jesus upon the earth:

1. **There must be a successful reign of man and the Last Adam (Jesus) from and over the realm—earth—where God tasked the first Adam to rule.**

Eschatology (i.e. last things) fits perfectly with protology (i.e. first things). Premillennialism best coincides with what God first tasked man to do—successfully rule the earth. In Gen 1:26–28 God told man to "rule" and "subdue" the "very good" (v. 31) creation that God entrusted to him. Adam, who was made in God's image, was called to exercise authority over the earth and function as God's mediatorial and representative king over it. But Adam failed this task when he disobeyed God. When this happened mankind as a whole failed since Adam acted as our representative (see Rom 5:12d). But Paul speaks of Jesus as another representative of mankind, a "Last Adam" (see 1 Cor 15:45) who succeeds where the first Adam failed (see Rom 5:17).

Important patterns exist between Jesus and Adam. Jesus, at times, repeats the pattern of Adam, succeeding where Adam failed.

For example, Adam and Eve failed the temptation from Satan in Genesis 3, but Christ withstood and triumphed over the temptations of Satan (Matthew 4). With Romans 5, Adam's act of disobedience brought condemnation to all men (5:12) while Jesus' "one act of righteousness" (the cross) brought righteousness. As two federal heads of humanity, Adam brought death but Jesus brought life.

There is another important parallel between Adam and Jesus. Just as Adam was appointed as king to rule successfully from and over the earth, so too Jesus will successfully reign from and over the earth as King. In Matt 19:28, Jesus said that in the "regeneration" or "renewal" of the planet, He "will sit on His glorious throne" and the twelve apostles will be there with Him "judging the twelve tribes of Israel." This is kingdom-over-the-earth language (see also Rev 5:10).

The main point here is that Jesus as the Last Adam is destined to rule from and over the realm where the first Adam failed. With His first coming, Jesus exhibited His kingdom authority in the earthly realm many times with His nature miracles. When He walked on water, multiplied bread, healed diseases, and raised the dead, He showed His power in the realm of nature. These were tastes and glimpses of the kingdom conditions to come, a restored Eden and earth. But Rom 8:19–23 reveals that the full restoration of nature awaits the return of Jesus and the glorification of the saints. Today we still see decay, illness, death, natural disasters, famines, earthquakes, and many other calamities that let us know that nature is not yet subject to man (Heb 2:5–8), that the consequences of Adam's failure are still with us. But Jesus is coming again with His kingdom to fulfill the Adamic mandate over the earth. The earth will be restored (see Isaiah 11). Sung Wook Chung accurately connects the kingdom role of Jesus as the Last Adam with a rule over the earth:

> Therefore by establishing the millennial kingdom, Jesus Christ, as the last Adam, will restore and fulfill not only the spiritual/priestly dimension but also the physical/institutional dimension of the first Adam's kingdom.[1]

---

[1] Sung Wook Chung, "Toward the Reformed and Covenantal Theology of Premillennialism," in *A Case for Historic Premillennialism: An Alternative to 'Left Behind' Eschatology*, eds. Craig L. Blomberg and Sung Wook Chung (Grand Rapids: Baker, 2009), 142.

A great strength of premillennialism is that it is the only millennial view that places Jesus' messianic and millennial reign *from and over the earth*, and in doing so sees Jesus completing what was expected of Adam. Other millennial perspectives place the center of Jesus' reign from heaven, but heaven is not where God placed Adam to rule. Psalm 115:16 declares, "The heavens are the LORD's, but the earth He has given to the human race" (HCSB).

Also, the reign of the Last Adam is not just a spiritual rule. Amillennialism makes Jesus' messianic and millennial reign a spiritual kingdom now, either with the church or with deceased saints in heaven. But God did not create man to rule from heaven over a spiritual kingdom. He put him on earth to reign from earth. If premillennialism is not true, then there is no successful mediatorial reign of man and the Last Adam (Jesus) in the realm where the first Adam failed. The kingdom of the Last Adam is in a different sphere (heaven) over a different realm (spiritual). But this does not do justice to what the Bible says about the destiny of the Last Adam.

So then, premillennialism is the only millennial view that has Jesus succeeding in the realm where the first Adam failed. Chung puts it well:

> The first Adam's priest-kingly activity, which was thwarted by the fall, will be fulfilled in the millennial kingdom. Therefore the millennial kingdom will be a restoration and fulfillment of the Edenic kingdom on the earth.[2]

Adam → tasked to rule from and over the earth → FAILURE

Jesus (Last Adam) → tasked to rule from and over the earth → SUCCESS

2. Jesus must have a sustained and visible reign in the realm where He was rejected.

Since the fall of man in Genesis 3, God has enacted a plan to bring this rebel planet back into conformity with His will (see Gen

---

[2] Ibid., 143.

3:15). Central to this plan is God's Son, Jesus the Messiah, whom the Father wants to establish as King over the nations (see Psalm 2). Through the prophecies of the Old and New Testaments the Bible presents Jesus as the One who will bring salvation to God's people and the One who will reign as King over this world.

Yet while millions in history have bowed the knee to Jesus as Lord, Savior, and King, the vast majority of the world has not. They do not worship Jesus. Survey a world map and ask which countries are bowing the knee to Jesus the Messiah. There are none. The nations with their leaders are still in active rebellion against God's "Anointed One" (see Ps 2:2). We see this in the myriads of false religions and philosophies along with overt acts of rebellion that characterize what Paul called "this present evil age" (Gal 1:4).

While the church has accomplished much during its two-thousand year history, its existence has not led to global recognition of Jesus. Even geographical areas once permeated with gospel awareness, such as Europe during the Reformation, and the American Northeast with the Great Awakening, are far removed from worship of the true God. Northern Africa, once a center for Christianity, is now essentially barren of Christian witness. Some of the most anti-Christian areas today are those that once had much exposure to the gospel.[3]

Contrary to the claims of postmillennialists, there is no evidence from Scripture or experience that the appropriate honor due Jesus will occur before His second coming to earth. All Christians agree that such honor will be given with Jesus' return to earth. When Jesus returns to earth in glory, every eye will see Him. He will slay His enemies and there will be no doubt as to His power. On the other hand, it is also true, as 1 Cor 15:24–28 indicates, that when the "end" occurs, Jesus "hands over the kingdom to the God and Father" (v. 24). Verse 28 states, "When all things are subjected to Him [Jesus], then the Son Himself also will be subjected to the One who subjected all things to Him, so that God may be all in all." So a time is coming when Jesus will hand His kingdom over to the Father. This does not mean Jesus ceases to reign, but His messianic kingdom will transition to the universal kingdom of the Father.

---

[3] This point alone should be a concern for those considering the validity of postmillennialism, which affirms societal renewal by the gospel before the return of Jesus.

This leads to an issue that must be addressed. It is the Father's will that His Son rule the nations and that all be subjected to Him. But in this "present evil age" not all things are subject to Jesus. Also, the Bible tells us that Jesus will one day hand His kingdom over to God the Father. This appears to be the time period of the Eternal State. So the question is this—*When does Jesus the Messiah rule in His kingdom and receive the glory and honor in this world that He richly deserves and the Scripture promises?* Is it simply at His second coming to earth? Saucy asks this relevant question:

> To be sure, the world will recognize Christ when he returns in glory. But does a short period of destruction and judgment before he turns the kingdom over to the Father for the Eternal State provide an adequate explanation of the centrality of Christ and a sufficient manifestation of his glory *within history*?[4]

The correct answer to this question is, no. Jesus' second coming with its destruction and judgments is not all there is to His manifestation. The day of His coming is a magnificent display of glory, but more is to come. As Saucy notes, "So far in history, the experience of Christ and his people has been one of oppression and nonrecognition (cf. 1 Jn 3:1). If history comes to its end with the coming of Christ, there will be no significant time within history when his centrality is manifest."[5] So where does the needed recognition come from?

An intermediate or millennial kingdom before the Eternal State "provides just such a time when Christ's glory will pervade human history and His significance will be rightly recognized."[6] *Thus, a millennial reign of Jesus after His second coming but before the "end" when Jesus hands His kingdom over to the Father is the ideal time for the Son to be manifested in His glory to the world.* Therefore, the millennial kingdom of Jesus after His return will be the time period when the Son reigns over this world, rewarding His servants and punishing His enemies. When He has completed this reign from His glorious throne He will

---

[4] Robert L. Saucy, *The Case for Progressive Dispensationalism: The Interface between Dispensational and Non-Dispensational Theology* (Grand Rapids: Zondervan, 1993), 289–90.

[5] Ibid., 290.

[6] Ibid.

then hand His kingdom over to God the Father and the Eternal State will commence.

Perhaps one objection to this claim is that Jesus' current session in heaven, fulfills the idea of a sustained reign that the Bible predicted. This position, though, is not satisfactory and does not give justice to Jesus' kingdom reign for several reasons. First, although Jesus' exaltation to the right hand of the Father is a powerful display of glory to the courts of heaven and evil spiritual forces (see Eph 1:21–23), heaven is not the realm where God tasked Adam and mankind to rule from. God placed Adam on earth and it is from earth that the Last Adam needs to reign.

Also, the world continues to escalate its rebellion and non-recognition of Jesus as Lord and Messiah. To be blunt, we cannot conceive of this present age as the full manifestation of Christ's kingdom. We cannot hold to a messianic reign of Christ where the vast majority of the world is not aware of it and is openly defiant to God. Yet this must be the case if the millennium is currently present. On the other hand, when Christ's kingdom is established at His coming it will be recognized by all. As Zech 14:9 indicates: "And the LORD will be king over all the earth; in that day the LORD will be the only one, and His name the only one." When Jesus the Messiah rules on the earth, there will be no other religions or false worship systems, unlike today. To put it in simpler terms, when Jesus is ruling, all will know it. Everyone will recognize it. His rule with a rod of iron will be respected (Ps 2:9; Rev 19:15).

Second, Heb 10:12–13 states that Jesus is at the right hand of God "waiting" for His enemies to be subjected to Him:

> but He, having offered one sacrifice for sins for all time, SAT DOWN AT THE RIGHT HAND OF GOD, waiting from that time onward UNTIL HIS ENEMIES BE MADE A FOOTSTOOL FOR HIS FEET (emphasis mine).

The wording here relies on Psalm 110 in which David's Lord, the Messiah, is said to have a session at the right hand of God "until" His enemies are defeated and the rule from Zion (Jerusalem) occurs (Ps 110:2). Thus, a session at the right hand of the Father by the Messiah precedes a kingdom reign upon the earth.

Next, the reign of the Messiah includes more than personal salvation, as important as that is. It also involves societal/political transformation for the nations of the earth (see Isa 2:2–4). International harmony under the ruling Messiah will occur as the government rests on His shoulders (Isa 9:6). While messianic salvation has been inaugurated in this present church age, the promised transformation of societies in all their dimensions has not happened yet. Passages like Isa 19:24–25 and Zech 14 predict that nations as national entities will worship God. But such societal and international harmony has not happened yet. How can there be a messianic or millennial reign in which the nations continue in open rebellion against God and His Messiah? The best answer is that this societal transformation will occur with the second coming of Jesus. As Saucy points out:

> The prophets pictured the saving work of the Messiah as both personal and societal renewal. The kingdom work of Christ has entered this age to bring personal salvation, but the transformation of society in terms of peace among peoples and the expression of God's righteousness in the structures of human society are never promised for this age. They await the return of the messianic King, who will destroy the evil structures of this age and institute a righteous rule over the earth for the first time in human history.[7]

To summarize, Jesus must be honored with a kingdom reign that is visible to all. God's intent is for His Son, Jesus the Messiah, to rule the nations, including His enemies, from Jerusalem and a restored Israel (see Ps 110:2). Before the perfect Eternal State comes, Jesus must rule over this planet that has rejected God since the Fall and over the world that rejected Him at His first coming. He will rule with righteousness but also with a rod of iron over His enemies (see Pss 2; 110; Rev 2:26–27). While Jesus is currently at the right hand of God in heaven possessing all authority, the nations are still currently in rebellion against God. There is no national entity today that acknowledges and worships God as they should. But that will change when Jesus comes again. At His second coming Jesus will then sit on His glorious throne (see Matt 19:28 and 25:31), and He will rule over this world to the glory of God. This He does in the millennial kingdom after He returns to earth. When this phase of the

---

[7] Saucy, *The Case for Progressive Dispensationalism*, 290.

kingdom program is over, the Son will hand the kingdom over to God the Father and the millennial kingdom will merge into the universal kingdom (see 1 Cor 15:24–28; Rev 22:1).

Look at this issue from another direction. If the premillennial view is *not* correct and the millennium is spiritual and now as amillennialism claims, what would this mean? It would mean that there will be no significant period in human history where Jesus is recognized as King by this world before the Eternal State. The present age is characterized by wickedness and persecution of God's people by the world and Satan. Also, Jesus' messianic reign would be characterized by non-recognition and continual widespread rebellion by the nations. In addition, while a present millennium would include personal salvation of some, it would not involve societal transformation and international harmony that the Bible predicted (see Isa 2:2–4). If the premillennial view is not correct there is no significant period in history where Jesus is given the honor and glory that He deserves. Premillennialism is Christ-honoring in that it sees, as necessary, a sustained and recognized reign of Jesus in His glory in the realm where He was rejected.

Jesus' first coming → Rejection of Jesus on earth

Jesus' second coming → Vindication and reign of Jesus on earth

---

3. There must be a vindication and reign of the saints in the realm where they were persecuted

The Bible reveals that the period before the Messiah's kingdom is one of persecution and opposition for the saints from both the world and Satan. The blood of the martyrs throughout history and the abuse of God's people in many lands confirms this fact.

The millennial kingdom of the Messiah, though, is presented as a reversal of these difficult conditions on earth. So in addition to looking at how the millennium relates to Jesus, it is also important to examine what the millennium means for Jesus' servants. The millennium is a time of vindication and reigning for God's saints in the realm where they were persecuted. With the millennium there will be an ironic reversal of roles. God turns the tables on His enemies who persecute His people and flips the experience of believers. God's people who now are persecuted by Satan and the nations, will be rewarded, vindicated, and given authority over the nations on earth. They go from persecution to reigning. *Thus, a future millennial kingdom is necessary for the reward and vindication of God's people in the realm where there were persecuted.*

Daniel 7

Such a reversal of circumstances for the saints is found in Daniel 7. This chapter tells of the messianic figure called "the Son of Man" (Jesus) who is presented before the "Ancient of Days" (the Father) and granted "dominion, glory, and a kingdom" (Dan 7:13–14). We are then told of the evil ministry of a "horn" who is a world leader rising from the midst of ten other leaders ("horns") (Dan 7:8, 20). This "horn" offers great boasts and persecutes the saints of God. But this persecution is only for a time until God intervenes:

> I kept looking, and that horn was waging war with the saints and overpowering them until the Ancient of Days came and judgment was passed in favor of the saints of the Highest One, and the time arrived when the saints took possession of the kingdom (Dan 7:21–22).

This enemy of God's people prevails for a while. He was "overpowering them," but God intervenes on the saints' behalf. When God does this "judgment was passed in favor of the saints," and they "took possession of the kingdom." This is a dramatic reversal of circumstances. Persecution leads to vindication. To use a boxing analogy, just when the people of God seemed on the ropes and then out for the count, a knockout of the enemy occurs and God's people are the victors with hands raised in victory.

Notice that the saints were not reigning when the "horn" was waging war against them on earth. But when God intervenes with judgment and His kingdom comes, the roles are reversed and the enemy is defeated, and God's people are the ones in charge. This is an ironic reversal of power. This scenario is further amplified in Dan 7:25–27:

He [the horn] will speak out against the Most High and wear down the saints of the Highest One, and he will intend to make alterations in times and in law; and they will be given into his hand for a time, times, and half a time. But the court will sit for judgment, and his dominion will be taken away, annihilated and destroyed forever. <u>Then the sovereignty, the dominion and the greatness of all the kingdoms under the whole heaven will be given to the people of the saints of the Highest One</u>; His kingdom will be an everlasting kingdom, and all the dominions will serve and obey Him.

When the Son of Man (Jesus) begins His kingdom given to Him by the Ancient of Days (see Dan 7:13–14), the saints of God will have an active role in this kingdom. God and Jesus are the Kings, but they share their kingdom with those who serve them. *The major point is that God's people are persecuted for a time, but when Messiah's kingdom comes, reward and vindication come with it and the enemy is destroyed.* This is not occurring now in this age but it will in the coming kingdom. Also, there is no indication that this reign of the saints is in heaven. The saints were persecuted on earth and their reign will be upon the earth as well (Rev 5:10).

Revelation 2–3

The pattern of tribulation followed by vindication and reward is affirmed in Revelation 2–3. As Jesus addressed His churches, each is evaluated for its performance. Then they are left with promises of future blessings for persevering during present trials. Faithfulness now leads to future blessings:

- <u>Ephesus</u>: right to eat of the tree of life in the Paradise of God (2:7)
- <u>Smyrna</u>: will not be hurt by the second death (2:11)
- <u>Pergamum</u>: given hidden manna, a white stone, and a new name written on the stone (2:17)
- <u>Thyatira</u>: granted authority and rule over the nations (2:26–27)
- <u>Sardis</u>: clothed in white garments, name in book of life, and name confessed before the Father and the angels (3:5–6)

- Philadelphia: given pillar in the temple of God; the name of God and the New Jerusalem (3:12)
- Laodicea: sit with Jesus on His throne (3:21)

There is a noticeable pattern here. Jesus' churches are facing difficult times. These are not days of reigning but of holding fast during Satanic persecution. Some churches are doing better than others, but all of them need encouragement. So Jesus offers rewards as motivation for faithful service. These rewards are not the current experience of these churches. But they will be received with Jesus' return to earth and the establishment of His kingdom. Jesus does not tell the churches that His kingdom is currently in operation or that the kingdom is their present experience. Instead, His message is about remaining faithful so that they can reap the blessings of the coming kingdom reign. Jesus' message to Thyatira highlights this point:

> He who overcomes, and he who keeps My deeds until the end, TO HIM I WILL GIVE AUTHORITY OVER THE NA-TIONS; AND HE SHALL RULE THEM WITH A ROD OF IRON, AS THE VESSELS OF THE POTTER ARE BROKEN TO PIECES, as I also have received authority from My Father (Rev 2:26–27).

Jesus uses Psalm 2, which describes the announcement that God's King, who is also His Son, will rule over the rebellious nations. The message of Psalm 2 is that the nations who scorn God now will one day have to submit to Him through His Messiah. With Rev 2:26–27 Jesus states that when His kingdom reign begins He will share and delegate His authority with those who are part of His church. In an ironic reversal of circumstances, the persecuted ones will one day become those who rule. So when the Messiah rules, those who belong to Him also participate in this rule. The kingdom is future and the saints' participation in this kingdom reign is also future. Jesus also promises a future kingdom rule as a reward in Rev 3:21:

> He who overcomes, I will grant to him to sit down with Me on My throne, as I also overcame and sat down with My Father on His throne.

The overcomer is one who "will" (future tense) sit down with Jesus on His throne. Again, present faithfulness leads to future kingdom reward. So then, Rev 2:26–27 and 3:21 point the churches to a future time when they will reign with Jesus for faithful service now.

Another significant matter is how intense and pervasive Satan's opposition is to the churches of Revelation 2–3. Satan is mentioned five times (2:9, 13 [twice], 24; 3:9). The church at Smyrna was not only facing "tribulation" and "poverty," they had to deal with a "synagogue of Satan" (2:9). The church at Pergamum was holding firm in the area where "Satan's throne is" (2:13).[8] The church at Thyatira had withstood "the deep things of Satan" (2:24). The church at Philadelphia also had to face a "synagogue of Satan" (3:9).

The churches of Revelation are characterized by persecution and opposition from Satan. The churches are not reigning or experiencing the kingdom of Christ yet. Positionally they are the nucleus for that coming kingdom (see Rev 1:6), but the promises of reward and vindication are future. Also, Satan is not bound since he is very active in opposing the people of God. This point alone casts doubt on the positions of amillennialism and postmillennialism that assert that Satan is bound in this age. This is not the case according to Revelation 2–3.

Revelation 11:15 announces the coming of the seventh trumpet judgment. It is at this time that loud voices in heaven declare, "The kingdom of the world has become the kingdom of our Lord and of His Christ; and He will reign forever and ever" (11:15b). Verses 17–18 indicate how this kingdom reign relates to judgment and the rewarding of God's people. The twenty-four elders declare:

"We give You thanks, O Lord God, the Almighty, who are and who were, because You have taken Your great power and have begun to reign. And the nations were enraged, and Your wrath came, and the time came for the dead to be judged, and the time to reward Your bond-servants the prophets and the saints and those who fear Your name, the small and the great, and to destroy those who destroy the earth."

---

[8] The reference to "Satan's throne" seems problematic for the amillennial and postmillennial views that claim a current binding of Satan in this age. How can Satan have a throne and be bound at the same time? Did Satan take his thrown to the abyss?

Again, as with Rev 2:26–27 and 3:21, this passage points to the rewarding of God's people. This "was the time to reward your bond-servants the prophets and the saints and those who fear Your name." The coming of the kingdom brings reward.

Revelation 20:4

With Rev 20:1–6 the promised resurrection, reward, and vindication of the saints occurs. Satan is imprisoned and swept away from the world to the abyss (Rev 20:1–3). And then in verse 4 we are told:

> Then I saw thrones, and they sat on them, and judgment was given to them. And I saw the souls of those who had been beheaded because of their testimony of Jesus and because of the word of God, and those who had not worshiped the beast or his image, and had not received the mark on their forehead and on their hand; and they came to life and reigned with Christ for a thousand years.

The words "I saw thrones, and they sat on them, and judgment was given to them," appear to have a connection with Dan 7:22 and its statement that "judgment was passed in favor of the saints of the Highest One, and the time arrived when the saints took possession of the kingdom." It also connects with Dan 7:27: "Then the sovereignty, the dominion and the greatness of all the kingdoms under the whole heaven will be given to the people of the saints of the Highest One." The promised vindication of the saints with the kingdom of the Son of Man discussed in Daniel 7 is fulfilled with the reign of the saints in the millennial kingdom of Rev 20:1–6.

Revelation 20:4 is a beautiful depiction of the coming reversal of circumstances for the saints of God. They are resurrected and on thrones with the authority to rule in the kingdom. Such circumstances have not occurred yet but they will when Jesus comes again to earth.

To summarize, a millennial kingdom after the return of Jesus is necessary for there to be a true reward and vindication of the saints of God. Such reward and vindication awaits a future fulfillment. As Dave Mathewson states:

The period of the church age is one in which the kingdom of God and the saints is contested by Satan and his kingdom . . . The authority of the beast is acknowledged worldwide (13:3–4) and God's people appear defeated (chaps. 11, 13). Moreover, the beast has apparently survived a fatal blow (13:3–4). *However, the millennium reverses this situation by providing a counterpart to the beast's earthly sovereignty and ostensible invincibility.* The dragon, Satan, is bound and the dragon and beast are thrown into the lake of fire (19:20; 20:1–3, 7–11). Now the saints triumph and they reign and rule, and for a comparably much longer period of time, one thousand years.[9]

The thousand-year kingdom, therefore, "portrays the complete victory and vindication of the saints at the Parousia of Christ."[10]

Consider this point from the opposite direction. If premillennialism is not true and the millennium is today, then the reward and vindication of the saints is taking place in this present evil age, which is difficult to believe and goes against our experiences. For example, Paul chided the Corinthians for thinking they were reigning already (see 1 Cor 4:8) and instead described his situation: "To this present hour we are both hungry and thirsty, and are poorly clothed, and are roughly treated, and are homeless. . . . we have become as the scum of the world, the dregs of all things, even until now" (1 Cor 4:11, 13).

Also, note that the souls of the martyrs who appear in heaven in Rev 6:9–11 are not vindicated or reigning yet in the world but are told to "rest for a little while longer" until God's vengeance takes care of their enemies. The vindication of these martyrs occurs in the millennium of Rev 20:4, where we are told "they came to life and reigned with Christ for a thousand years." The martyred saints persecuted on earth later become the resurrected and rewarded saints reigning on earth. The reward and vindication of the saints fits better with the second coming of Jesus and the kingdom He brings.

---

[9] Dave Mathewson, "A Re-examination of the Millennium in Rev 20:1–6: Consummation and Recapitulation" *Journal of the Evangelical Theological Society* 44, no. 2 (June 2001): 248. Emphases mine.

[10] Ibid.

> Present age: Saints are persecuted on earth as they serve Jesus.
>
> Millennial kingdom: Saints are rewarded on earth for faithful service.

4. **There needs to be a time in history where all aspects of the covenants and promises are fulfilled**

The Christian church has affirmed two comings of Jesus. The first occurred in the first century A.D., and the second will occur on a future day. There are certain things we should expect in regard to the fact that there are two comings of Jesus. One is that certain prophecies and promises were fulfilled with Jesus' first coming, while others await fulfillment at His second coming. If Jesus' coming has two parts to it, then it makes sense that the fulfillment of matters related to Him would come in stages as well.

The first coming of Jesus brought the ultimate Son of David (Jesus) and His sacrificial death. The first coming also brought messianic salvation to believing Jews and Gentiles and the New Covenant ministry of the Holy Spirit. Yet the Bible also indicates that there are major aspects of prophecy that still need to be fulfilled. For example, in Acts 1:6, the apostles asked Jesus, "Lord, is it at this time you are restoring the kingdom to Israel?" The apostles did not view Israel's promised restoration as occurring yet. That's why they asked the Lord when it would occur (see also Deut 30:1–6; Ezekiel 36; Rom 11:26–27). In 2 Thessalonians 2 Paul explains why the Day of the Lord had not started yet. The dimensions of Israel's land boundaries described in Gen 15:18–21 still need to be fulfilled. The restoration of the city of Jerusalem has not happened yet (see Jer 31:38–40; Luke 21:24). Harmony among nations needs to occur (see Isa 2:2–4). Restoration of the animal kingdom in Messiah's kingdom needs to be realized (see Isaiah 11). In sum, many of the national and physical promises of the Bible are unfulfilled currently.

So then, unfulfilled prophecy is a major reason why there must be a millennium. The millennium is the ideal time period when unfulfilled prophecies and promises will be fulfilled. If God is true and cannot lie, we know that all aspects of His promises will come to fruition with the coming kingdom.

A couple of objections could be offered against this point. One may be that Jesus has already fulfilled all the prophecies, covenants, and promises of the Old Testament. After all, doesn't Paul say that all the promises are "Yes" in Jesus (see 2 Cor 1:20). Doesn't Jesus says that He came to fulfill the Law and the Prophets? (see Matt 5:17).

The correct answer is that Jesus does fulfill all that was promised. But the real issue is "how" and "when" He fulfills these matters. Does He fulfill them by having them spiritually absorbed into Himself or by fulfilling physical promises in a spiritual way? Or does He fulfill them by being the One through whom the literal fulfillment of God's promises come true? The latter is the better option. Jesus is the center of God's kingdom plans. Jesus is at the center of God's promise plan (see Gen 3:15). Without Him God's kingdom and salvation plan would never happen. But these fulfillments take place as a result of two comings of Jesus. To date we have never experienced harmony among nations, the restoration of the animal kingdom, the restoration of Israel to her land, etc. Can we simply spiritualize these and say they are already fulfilled in Jesus?

Second, the New Testament reaffirms many Old Testament prophecies that still need to occur, such as the Day of the Lord (2 Pet 3:10) and the appearance of the Antichrist (2 Thess 2:3–4). If Jesus fulfilled everything with His first coming, why do the New Testament writers view so many prophecies as still needing to be fulfilled?

Third, Jesus himself referred to many prophecies that still needed to be fulfilled, even after His first earthly ministry was near completion. In His Olivet Discourse (cf. Matthew 24–25; Luke 21), Jesus predicted many things that still needed to happen, such as the abomination of desolation, cosmic signs, the gathering of His people, and the judgment of the nations. Nowhere does He say that the details of these prophecies do not matter because they are absorbed into Him.

Another objection could be that unfulfilled prophecies and promises could be fulfilled in the Eternal State and not the millennium. However, there is a major problem with this objection. If the Eternal State is the fulfillment of yet unfulfilled promises, this means that these matters would come to fruition outside the mediatorial kingdom of Jesus the Messiah. Yet the Bible links fulfillment of many of these matters with Messiah's kingdom. For example, the restoration of the animal kingdom described in Isa 11:6–9 is linked with the coming Davidic ruler in 11:1 ("stem of Jesse").

If premillennialism is not true, then the unfulfilled prophecies of the Bible do not find fulfillment just as God promised. What the Old Testament writers intended and what their hearers understood were wrong. The prophecies have to be spiritualized, or absorbed into Jesus, or fulfilled in the Eternal State outside the realm of Messiah's kingdom. Whichever option is chosen, the fulfillment would not be like the literal fulfillments of the prophecies that occurred at Jesus' first coming. There would be an inconsistency in how God fulfills His promises. The better position is that God fulfills all of His promises just as He said and that unfulfilled prophecies will be fulfilled with Jesus' return and the millennial kingdom that the Messiah brings.

Jesus' first coming → many prophecies were literally fulfilled.

Jesus' second coming → prophecies not fulfilled at the first coming will be literally fulfilled.

8

PREMILLENNIALISM AND THE GOODNESS OF GOD'S CREATION

Historically, premillennialism has been an antidote against attempts to deny the importance of God's physical creation. The church has often battled encroaching forms of Platonism and its bias against material matters.

Platonism is a philosophy rooted in the ideas of the great ancient Greek philosopher, Plato (427–347 B.C.). Plato argued that reality is primarily ideal or abstract. With his 'theory of forms,' he asserted that ultimate reality is not found in objects and concepts that we experience on earth. Instead, reality is found in 'forms' or 'ideas' that transcend our physical world. These forms allegedly operate as perfect universal templates for everything we experience in the world. One result of Platonism was the belief that matter is inferior to the spiritual. Thus, there is a dualism between matter and the immaterial. This dualism, though, is not consistent with the Christian worldview which affirms the goodness of all aspects of God's creation. When God created the world he deemed it "very good" (Gen 1:31).

One religious form of Platonism was Gnosticism, which was one of the greatest foes of the church in the second and third centuries. Gnosticism promoted an unbiblical dualism between the spiritual and the physical—emphasizing the former and denigrating the latter. According to Donald Fairbairn, Gnostic dualism had four important results:

1. It led to the view that the material world is evil and unredeemable and that salvation applies only to the soul, not
the body.
2. It led to a denigration of history; if the physical world is
unredeemable then the panorama of history played out in
the physical world is of little consequence.
3. It led to a distinction in gods—the lesser, material god of
the Old Testament and the higher, spiritual God of the
New Testament.
4. It led to a docetic view of Christ in which Christ only appears to be human and fleshly.[1]

How did the church fight these heretical ideas? Premillennialism
was an important weapon against encroaching Gnosticism. Donald
Fairbairn points out that, "the church fathers who led this battle—
Irenaeus and Tertullian—used their premillennialism as a primary
weapon."[2]

In this battle with Gnosticism, Irenaeus (second century A.D.)
wanted to demonstrate the unity of Scripture and show that the Old
Testament and New Testament worked in harmony. This "is what
drives him into the details of Daniel and Revelation."[3] Fairbairn also
points out that "behind Irenaeus's treatment of an earthly kingdom
lies the concern to refute the gnostic denigration of the material
world."[4] In Irenaeus's mind, "nothing could be more appropriate for
the God who created the world and redeemed humanity through
early history than to conclude his work with an earthly kingdom as a
transition to an eternal kingdom that will also be on a refurbished
earth."[5] Irenaeus believed that anyone who denied an earthly kingdom as being too sensuous or not "spiritual" enough was denying
the goodness of God who created the physical universe.[6]

---

[1] Donald Fairbairn, "Contemporary Millennial/Tribulational Debates," *A
Case for Historic Premillennialism: An Alternative to "Left Behind" Eschatology*, ed. Craig L.
Blomberg and Sung Wook Chung (Grand Rapids: Baker, 2009), 129.

[2] Ibid.

[3] Ibid.

[4] Ibid.

[5] Ibid.

[6] Ibid., 130.

A. Skevington Wood also affirms that premillennialism was a weapon used by Irenaeus against the Gnostics:

> It ought also to be borne in mind that the strong emphasis of Irenaeus on the literal fulfillment of the prophecies concerning the Millennium were no doubt conditioned to some degree by the fact that he was contending against the gnostic heretics, who denied the redeemability of the material. The millennial teaching of Irenaeus must not be isolated from the rest of his theology. It is all of a piece with it, and Irenaeus was the first to formulate (however embryonically) a millennial—indeed premillennial—system of interpretation.[7]

For Irenaeus, the significance of eschatology was not simply in knowing the details of what will happen in the end times. Instead, "eschatology's significance lies in the way it testifies to the unity of Scripture, the unity of God's purposes, and ultimately the unity and goodness of the God we worship."[8] For Irenaeus and most of the church before Origen,

> an earthly kingdom following the return of Christ is not merely what Revelation 20 teaches. It is also a central tenet of the faith because it functions to reinforce the central truths of Christianity—that there is one God who in love has created this world for us and us for it, who has personally entered this world in order to redeem us for a future in this world, and who will ultimately triumph in this world over the forces that are arrayed against him.[9]

Fairbairn laments that the battle against Gnosticism and overspiritualization tendencies has never been totally won. For him, "Perhaps part of the reason we have not won it is that we have forfeited the use of one of the greatest biblical/theological weapons in this battle—eschatology. Have we overspiritualized the hope held

---

[7] A. Skevington Wood, "The Eschatology of Irenaeus," *Evangelical Quarterly* 40 (1968): 36.

[8] Fairbairn, "Contemporary Millennial/Tribulational Debates," 130.

[9] Ibid.

out to Christians and thus essentially conceded to the Gnostics among us that the material world is not ultimately important?"[10] So premillennialism was and is a weapon against attempts to create an unbiblical dualism between the spiritual and the material. It functions as an antidote to over-spiritualized views of God's purposes.

This is not to say that other millennial views do not affirm the goodness of God's physical creation. Like premillennialists, both amillennialists and postmillennialists affirm a coming bodily resurrection and a tangible new earth.[11] Yet historically, amillennialism has stumbled in the area of spiritualizing material realities and has often been linked with Platonist tendencies of over-spiritualization of God's purposes. Augustine (354-430), known as the father of amillennialism, was heavily influenced by Platonism. According to Gary Habermas, "Christian thought also came under the influence of Platonism, as scholars of the third century such as Clement of Alexandria and Origen mixed this Greek philosophy with their theology. In particular, Augustine's interpretation of Plato dominated Christian thought for the next thousand years after his death in the fifth century."[12]

Augustine was also influenced by neo-Platonism which was a religious form of Platonism. As Viviano states, "we need only note that Augustine was strongly influenced by neo-Platonic philosophy and has even read Plotinus and Porphyry . . . . This philosophy was highly spiritual and other-worldly, centered on the one and the eternal, treating the material and the historically contingent as inferior stages in the ascent of the soul to union with the one."[13] Viviano

---

[10] Ibid., 131.

[11] As the amillennialist Robert E. Strimple states, "When we read modern amillennialists themselves, do we find them expressing a purely 'spiritual' (i.e. non-physical) eschatological hope? Not at all." Strimple, "An Amillennial Response to Craig A. Blaising," in *Three Views on the Millennium and Beyond*, ed. Darrell L. Bock (Grand Rapids: Zondervan, 1999), 257. He then lists a series of amillennial theologians who believe in a "more earth-oriented vision" of eschatology including Herman Bavinck, Geerhardus Vos, Anthony Hoekema, and Greg K. Beale. (259–60).

[12] Gary R. Habermas, "Plato, Platonism," *Evangelical Dictionary of Theology*, ed. Walter A. Elwell (Grand Rapids: Baker, 1984), 860. Allen states, "The Greek Fathers and Augustine drew most extensively on the philosophy of Plato and the Platonists." Diogenes Allen, *Philosophy for Understanding Theology* (Atlanta: John Knox, 1985), 91.

[13] Benedict T. Viviano, O.P. *The Kingdom of God in History* (Eugene, OR: Wipf and Stock, 1988), 52.

summarizes the impact of Augustine's Platonic thinking on his spiritual views of the kingdom of God:

> Thus Augustine was attracted to the spiritual interpretation of the kingdom we have already seen in Origen. Indeed, ultimately for Augustine, the kingdom of God consists in eternal life with God in heaven. That is the *civitas dei*, the city of God, as opposed to the *civitas terrena*.[14]

Augustine's spiritual view of the kingdom contributed to his belief that the period of the church on earth is the thousand-year reign of Christ spoken of in Revelation 20. According to Viviano, "Augustine's view would dominate and become the normal Roman Catholic view down to our own times."[15] It is difficult to deny the importance of Platonic thinking on the kingdom. Blaising rightly argues that a Platonic, spiritual vision model approach led to a rejection of the idea of an earthly kingdom:

> Ancient Christian premillennialism weakened to the point of disappearance when the spiritual vision model of eternity became dominant in the church. A future kingdom on earth simply did not fit well in an eschatology that stressed personal ascent to a spiritual realm.[16]

Augustine's spiritual presuppositions were behind his belief that the millennium of Rev 20:1–10 is being fulfilled spiritually through the institutional church in the present age.[17] On the other hand, premillennialism thrives in an environment where the goodness of the physical realm is affirmed. All Christians should be grateful that men like Irenaeus and others were able to use premillennialism as a weapon to fight over-spiritualized views of God's purposes. Premillennialism is important to the Christian worldview.

---

[14] Ibid., 52–53.

[15] Ibid., 54.

[16] Blaising, "Premillennialism," in *Three Views on the Millennium and Beyond*, 170.

[17] Ibid., 172–74.

9

PREMILLENNIALISM IN 1 CORINTHIANS 15

This book has tried to establish that premillennialism is true from various Old and New Testament passages. One Bible chapter that is sometimes pointed to as evidence against premillennialism is 1 Corinthians 15. For example, in his book, *Kingdom Come: The Amillennial Alternative*, amillennialist Sam Storms asserted that 1 Corinthians 15 presents insurmountable obstacles for the premillennial view.[1]

In summary, Storms argues three main points. First, he claims that 1 Cor 15:20–28 speaks of a two-stage resurrection program of God that leaves no room for an intermediate/millennial reign of Jesus where sin and death occur after the second coming. Second, he argues that Paul's statement in 1 Cor 15:50 that non-glorified bodies cannot enter God's kingdom makes premillennialism impossible since premillennialism requires the presence of non-glorified people in the millennium. And third, Storms believes that 1 Cor 15:50–57 teaches that the final conquering of death occurs with Jesus' second coming and not a thousand years after Jesus' return.

This chapter will argue that 1 Corinthians 15 is not a defeater of premillennialism, and that these three objections against premillennialism are not successful. In fact, 1 Corinthians 15 corresponds well with the premillennial view and the progression of the resurrection program offered in Rev 20:4–5. In short, a close study of 1 Corinthians 15 should lead one to a premillennial view.

---

[1] Sam Storms, *Kingdom Come: The Amillennial Alternative* (Ross-shire, Scotland: Mentor, 2013), 143–52.

The methodology of this chapter will focus on explaining 1 Corinthians 15, especially verses 20–28 and 50. As we do this we will address the three objections against premillennialism mentioned above. As 1 Corinthians 15 is interpreted in context, the three objections will be shown to be invalid.

The Three-Stage Resurrection Program

We begin with 1 Cor 15:20–28. A proper interpretation of this passage depends upon several things, including an understanding of key terms and quotations of Old Testament passages. Paul offers an "order" of God's resurrection program. Paul begins by pointing out that Christ's resurrection is "the first fruits of those who are asleep" (15:20). Since Jesus is raised from the dead, so too will those who are in Him. Then in 1 Cor 15:22–24 Paul declares:

> For as in Adam all die, so also in Christ all will be made alive. But each in his own order: Christ the first fruits, after that those who are Christ's at His coming, then comes the end, when He hands over the kingdom to the God and Father, when He has abolished all rule and all authority and power.

Here Paul gives a timeline of the "order" of the resurrection by pointing out three events and their relation to the kingdom. First, he says that Christ is "the first fruits" (v. 23a). This is a reference to the bodily resurrection of Christ. Christ's resurrection is the pattern and the guarantee that the resurrection of others will occur.

Second, "after that" there is a resurrection of "those who are Christ's at His coming" (v. 23b). This second stage is future from Paul's standpoint, who is writing in the 50s about twenty years after the resurrection of Jesus. When Jesus returns, those who belong to Him will be resurrected. From our standpoint in history, at least two-thousand years separates the first and second phases of the resurrection program. Third, Paul states, "Then comes the end," when Jesus "hands over the kingdom to the God the Father" (24a). This period of "the end" is another stage, a third phase in the resurrection program. To summarize, there are three stages of the resurrection according to 1 Cor 15:23–24a:

1. "Christ the first fruits"
2. "after that those who are Christ's at His coming"
3. "then comes the end . . . ."

While there is not much debate concerning the first two stages, there is considerable disagreement concerning the "end" and whether this is a third stage of the resurrection order or not. Those who hold a premillennial view believe Paul's words ("then comes the end") indicate a significant period of time between events 2 and 3. So an era exists between the resurrection of those at Christ's coming and the "end" when Jesus hands the kingdom over to God the Father. The "end" does not occur immediately after Jesus returns but occurs after the millennial kingdom reign of Jesus, the millennium that is discussed in Rev 20:1–6. As Craig Blaising argues, "Christ's coming marks the second stage, not the third (in which the end occurs)."[2]

On the other hand, those who do not agree with an intermediate kingdom of Christ after His second coming assert that "the end" follows immediately after Jesus' coming. For them, "the end" occurs as a result of the second coming of Christ. There is no third stage of the resurrection program and no room for an intermediate kingdom or millennium after Jesus' return. When Jesus returns and His people are resurrected the end comes at that time and the Eternal State begins.[3]

So which understanding is correct? Our view is that Paul is telling of a three-stage resurrection program that leaves room for a kingdom reign between Jesus' return and the "end," the kind of kingdom that John speaks of in Rev 20:1–6. Let us explain.

First, Paul's use of the term "order" (*tagma*) seems to hint at a progression of more than two stages. The word originally referred to order within a military context such as an order of troops. While an "order" of events could apply to only two resurrections, more than two is likely.

---

[2] Craig A. Blaising, "A Premillennial Response," in *Three Views on the Millennium and Beyond*, ed. Darrell L. Bock (Grand Rapids: Zondervan, 1999), 79.

[3] For a detailed defense of this view see Sam Storms, *Kingdom Come*, 143–48.

Second, a considerable gap of time certainly exists between the first and second resurrections, which makes a gap between the second and third possible. From our standpoint in history, at least two thousand years separates these two events.

A third reason involves Paul's use of the words *epeita* and *eita*, which are related to "after that" and "then." Before looking at the details of this argument, the main point we are making is this—Paul's use of *epeita* and *eita* in 1 Corinthians 15 is best understood as teaching an interval of time between the second coming of Jesus and "the end" when Jesus hands the kingdom over to the Father. This allows for a millennial reign of Jesus.

With 1 Cor 15:23 Paul refers to Christ as the "firstfruits" of the resurrection and then uses the temporal adverb *epeita* ("afterward") to then discuss the resurrection of those who belong to Christ at His coming. Then, in what D. Edmond Hiebert has referred to as "the crux of the millennial issue,"[4] Paul begins verse 24 with the indefinite phrase, *eita to telos* ("then comes the end"). The temporal adverb *eita* "likely implies an interval time between the coming of Christ and the end."[5] Matthew Waymeyer, in his study of the term *eita*, points out that this term often is used in contexts where an interval of time follows this term:

> Outside 1 Corinthians 15:24, the adverb εἶτα is used 14 times in the New Testament, 13 of which introduce something that occurs next in a sequence of events. Of these 13 temporal uses of εἶτα, five introduce an event that happens immediately after the previous event (Mark 8:25; Luke 8:12; John 13:5; 19:27; 20:27); six introduce an event that occurs after an interval of time between the two events (Mark 4:17; 4:28 [2x]; 1 Cor 15:5,

---

[4] D. Edmond Hiebert, "Evidence from 1 Corinthians 15," in *A Case for Premillenialism: A New Consensus*, eds. Donald K. Campbell and Jeffrey L. Townsend (Chicago: Moody, 1992), 229.

[5] Ibid., 230. Leon Morris states that *"Then (eita)* does not necessarily mean 'immediately after'. It indicates that what follows takes place at some unspecified time after the preceding." Leon Morris, *1 Corinthians*, Tyndale New Testament Commentaries (Grand Rapids: Eerdmans, 1985), 211.

7; 1 Tim 2:13); and once there may or may not be an intervening gap of time in view (1 Tim 3:10).[6]

This leads Waymeyer to conclude that *eita* "is often used to denote events separated by an interval of time, this in fact being Paul's most common use of the temporal adverb."[7]

So from a grammatical standpoint it is significant that *eita* often refers to an interval between two events. Just as there is a considerable time gap between Christ's resurrection and the resurrection of those who belong to Jesus (events 1 and 2), there could be a time gap between the resurrection of the people of God and the end when Jesus hands the kingdom over to the Father (events 2 and 3).

This understanding is also supported by a similar *epeita . . . eita* formula earlier in the chapter. In 1 Cor 15:5–8 Paul lays out a chronological order of events concerning Jesus' resurrection appearances. After stating that Jesus was raised on the third day (v. 4) he says,

and that He appeared to Cephas, then [*eita*] to the twelve. After that [*epeita*] He appeared to more than five hundred brethren at one time, most of whom remain until now, but some have fallen asleep; then [*epeita*] He appeared to James, then [*eita*] to all the apostles; and last of all, as to one untimely born, He appeared to me also.

No doubt exists that Paul is offering a chronological progression of resurrection appearances,[8] and he uses *epeita* and *eita* to reveal a progression of appearances. Verse 7 is particularly significant since, like 1 Cor 15:23b–24a, this verse also offers the *epeita . . . eita* formula and shows chronological progression with a time gap. Jesus appeared to James and then appeared to all the apostles.[9] In both cases the formula indicates a similar time gap:

---

[6] Matthew William Waymeyer, "A Biblical Critique of the Two-Age Model as an Argument against Premillennialism," Ph.D. diss., The Master's Seminary, 2015, 168-69.

[7] Ibid., 169.

[8] "He [Paul] indicates that he is listing the appearances in chronological order. . . ." Roy E. Ciampa and Brian S. Rosner, *The First Letter to the Corinthians*, The Pillar New Testament Commentary (Grand Rapids: Eerdmans, 2010), 749.

[9] Ciampa and Rosner point out that Christ appears to two individuals who are leaders of two groups. Jesus appears to Peter and then the group that Peter is

1 Cor 15:7: *epeita . . . eita* indicates a time gap of days

1 Cor 15:23b–24a: *epeita . . . eita* indicates a time gap of which we now know includes thousands of years (at least two thousand—one thousand).[10]

The fact that that the *epeita . . . eita* formula indicates a gap of similar time in 1 Cor 5:7 (days) reveals the likelihood that the formula in 1 Cor 15:23b–24a also indicates a gap of similar time (many years). Remember, that the main issue is whether the *epeita . . . eita* formula allows or indicates a time gap between the resurrection of those at the time of Jesus' coming and the "end." The evidence indicates that it does, not only from the immediate context of 1 Cor 15:22–24, but from a similar grammatical construction in 1 Cor 15:5–8.

In sum, 1 Cor 15:22–24 reveals a three-stage resurrection program with a gap of time between the second and third stages that allows for a considerable period of time for a kingdom reign of Jesus before the "end" comes. This answers the first objection against premillennialism mentioned in this chapter, namely that Paul is speaking of only two stages in the resurrection program that does not allow for a millennial kingdom after the return of Jesus. The evidence indicates a gap between the return of the Jesus and "the end" allowing for such a millennial kingdom of Jesus.

The Successful Earthly Reign of the Son before the Eternal State

Not only does Paul give significant information about the kingdom in regard to the resurrection program, he also states how the kingdom program relates to the Son. This involves a successful earthly reign of the Son before He hands the kingdom to the Father. As 1 Cor 15:24b–28 shows, the Father has a mission for Jesus, and when Jesus fulfills this mission a transition takes place in the kingdom program:

---

the leader of—the twelve. Likewise, Jesus appears to James and then the "slightly enlarged group of apostles" related to him in Jerusalem. (749).

[10] The "one thousand" is taking into account the thousand-year period mentioned several times in Rev 20:1–10.

then comes the end, when He hands over the kingdom to the God and Father, when He has abolished all rule and all authority and power. For He must reign until He has put all His enemies under His feet. The last enemy that will be abolished is death. For HE HAS PUT ALL THINGS IN SUBJECTION UNDER HIS FEET. But when He says, "All things are put in subjection," it is evident that He is excepted who put all things in subjection to Him. When all things are subjected to Him, then the Son Himself also will be subjected to the One who subjected all things to Him, so that God may be all in all.

When "the end" comes Jesus will hand the kingdom over to God the Father (1 Cor 15:24). So there comes a point when the kingdom reign of Jesus is followed by a handing of His kingdom over to the Father. *Some transition occurs.* This transition happens, though, only after the Son has "abolished all rule and all authority and power." So Jesus must reign and stamp out all opposition and then the eternal kingdom can begin. Any authority or power that is opposed to God must be fully and finally dealt with. Paul uses two Old Testament passages—Psalm 110 and Psalm 8—to reveal that he is referring to a future earthly reign of Jesus.

With 15:25 Paul says, "He must reign until He has put all His enemies under His feet" (25). The "must" means it is necessary that Jesus reigns. Paul's wording in verse 25 is a reference to Ps 110:1–2, which states:

> The LORD says to my Lord:
> "Sit at My right hand
> Until I make Your enemies a footstool for Your feet."
> The LORD will stretch forth Your strong scepter from Zion, saying,
> "Rule in the midst of Your enemies."

This allusion to Ps 110:1–2 is evidence that the "reign" of Jesus is a future earthly reign. The context of Psalm 110 is David's Lord, the Messiah, sitting at the right hand of God for a session in heaven "until" He begins His earthly reign over His enemies from "Zion" in Jerusalem. In reference to Ps 110:1, the author of Hebrews says that Jesus is "waiting" at the right hand of the Father (see Heb 10:12–13). When the heavenly session from the Father's throne is over,

God installs His Messiah on the earth to reign over it from Jerusalem. From our current historical perspective, Jesus is currently at the right hand of God the Father but this will be followed by a reign upon the earth. Thus, Jesus "must" reign from earth because Psalm 110 says this must happen. In Acts 3:21, Peter also uses "must" in regard to Jesus and His heavenly session before He returns to earth to restore everything:

> whom heaven <u>must</u> receive until the period of restoration of all things about which God spoke by the mouth of His holy prophets from ancient time (emphasis is mine).

Peter's point is that heaven must receive Jesus "until" the "period of the restoration of all things" occurs. This restoration has not occurred yet, but it will when Jesus returns to earth (see Acts 3:20). What Peter speaks of is similar to Paul's point in 1 Cor 15:25.

Note also that there is a "reign" of Jesus. This "reign" involves more than the second coming event (see Rev 19:11–21). The second coming is a swift event, but a "reign" involves considerable period of time. Jesus the Son and Messiah must have a sustained reign in the realm where the first Adam failed (see Gen 1:26, 28; 1 Cor 15:45).

With 15:27, Paul quotes Ps 8:6: "For HE HAS PUT ALL THINGS IN SUBJECTION UNDER HIS FEET." Paul is interpreting Ps 8:6 both literally and christologically. The psalm originally refers to man's right to rule God's creation. So how does this apply to both mankind and Jesus? Corporate personality is in view here in which a special leader represents the many. Psalm 8 is addressed to man in a general sense, but since Jesus is the ultimate Man and Last Adam, He represents man. Both Jesus and mankind are in view. As Mark Stephen Kinzer notes, "The psalm is read in both an individual and a corporate sense."[11]

The use of Psalm 8 is further evidence that Paul is thinking of a future earthly reign of Jesus. Psalm 8 explains and expands upon Gen 1:26–28 and its truth that God created man to rule successfully over the earth. *The Last Adam, Jesus, must succeed from and over the realm where the first Adam failed—earth.* The Last Adam's destiny is not to

---

[11] Mark Stephen Kinzer, "'All Things Under His Feet': Psalm 8 in the New Testament and in Other Jewish Literature of Late Antiquity," Ph.D. diss., The University of Michigan, 1995, 261.

rule from heaven in a spiritual kingdom. Instead, He is to rule *from* and *over* the earth just like the first Adam was supposed to do. But unlike Adam, Jesus will succeed. Those who place Jesus' kingdom reign in this age from heaven over a spiritual kingdom are not giving justice to an important part of God's kingdom program—which is for man to reign over the earth as God originally tasked him to do. Jesus as the ultimate Man and representative of mankind will fulfill this task. A spiritual reign from heaven does not complete what God requires in Gen 1:26–28 and Psalm 8. God expects a successful reign over the earth and Jesus the Son will accomplish this task. Then He will hand this kingdom over to the Father.

With verse 28, Paul declares that all things will be subject to Jesus, yet he notes one exception—God the Father. The Father is the One who commissioned the Son to reign over the earth, so the Father is not subject to the Son. Paul then states that when everything has been subjected to Jesus, Jesus then willingly subjects Himself to the Father so that the Father can be "all in all." The language here finds a cultural parallel in a Roman emperor who sends a trusted general with the task of squashing and fixing a rebellion in the empire. The emperor would grant the full authority and force of Rome to the general who would act on his behalf. When the trusted general succeeded in his mission and vanquished the enemies, he would then return to the emperor, not to challenge the emperor, but to show his subjection to him. The general acted with the full authority of the emperor and when victory occurs, he returns in victorious yet humble submission to the one who commissioned him.

This is similar to what Jesus accomplishes on behalf of the Father. The Father commissions Jesus to conquer and restore this fallen world on His behalf, and when Jesus accomplishes this task He then will subject Himself to the Father. Jesus' mission is accomplished and the Father is pleased with His reign. Every square inch of the universe has been restored. At this point the reign of Jesus is followed by the universal reign of God the Father. This does not mean that Jesus ceases to reign. Revelation 11:15 says Jesus "will reign forever and ever." So as McClain notes, "This does not mean the end of our Lord's regal activity, but rather that from here onward in the unity of the Godhead He reigns with the Father as the eternal

Son."[12] Messiah's kingdom is then blended into the Father's universal kingdom. Jesus' prayer, "Thy kingdom come, Thy will be done, on earth as it is in heaven" (Matt 6:10) is fully accomplished. Jesus' kingdom does not end like earthly kingdoms do by defeat, but by fulfillment.

Let us look even more closely at the statements that the Son "hands over the kingdom to the God and Father" (v. 24), and "the Son Himself also will be subjected to the One [the Father] who subjected all things to Him, so that God may be all in all" (v. 28). *These statements indicate a distinction between the Son's kingdom and the Father's kingdom.* Of course, these two phases of the kingdom plan work in perfect harmony. It is the Father's will that the Son's kingdom happen and succeed. And it is the Son's desire to fulfill the Father's mandate for man to rule and subdue the world for God's glory. Yet there is a distinction. It is during the Son's reign that Jesus, the ultimate Man and King, fulfills all the prophecies, covenants, and promises concerning God's mediatorial kingdom program. When this occurs in its entirety then the eternal kingdom of the Father commences. This truth again indicates the need for an era that is distinct both from this present age and the eternal kingdom. One should not simply assume that unfulfilled promises awaiting fulfillment will be fulfilled in the Eternal State. In doing so this would put fulfillment outside of the reign of Jesus the Messiah, to whom the task of fulfillment belongs.[13]

In sum, 1 Cor 15:20–28 teaches us that there are three phases of the resurrection program and that Jesus' kingdom occurs between

---

[12] Alva J. McClain, *The Greatness of the Kingdom: An Inductive Study of the Kingdom of God* (Winona Lake, IN: BMH Books, 1959), 513.

[13] To offer an example, the amillennialist, Anthony Hoekema, rightly insisted that the promised harmony among nations promised in Isa 2:2–4 will occur in the future and is not being fulfilled in the church See Anthony A. Hoekema, *The Bible and the Future* (Grand Rapids: Eerdmans, 1979), 205–6. But Hoekema put its fulfillment in the Eternal State and not Jesus' millennial kingdom. Yet the prophecies of Isaiah are linked with the "child" and "son" upon which "the government will rest on His shoulders" (Isa 9:6). This refers to Jesus. He is the one who will rule the nations. With Hoekema's scenario the reign over the nations of Isa 2:2–4 would not take place under the direct reign of the Messiah in His millennial kingdom. But this goes against the message of Isaiah. It is better to view Isa 2:2–4 and other passages that are not fulfilled yet as coming to fulfillment in a coming, intermediate kingdom under the direct rule of the Messiah.

His return and the "end." At the time of the third phase of God's resurrection plan, which comes after the intermediate kingdom, Jesus will hand the kingdom over to God the Father. The Son fulfills the kingdom mandate given to man to rule over the earth, and when this occurs the transition to the Father's eternal kingdom begins.

As shown, the grammar of 1 Cor 15:20–28 indicates a future reign of Jesus after His second coming to earth. Yet the context of 1 Corinthians also strengthens this understanding. Paul viewed the kingdom reign as future in 1 Corinthians 4 and 6. With 1 Cor 4:8 he chided the Corinthians for thinking they were reigning already when they were not ("I wish that you had become kings so that we also might reign with you"). And in 1 Cor 6:2–3 he stated that the kingdom reign of the saints involves judging angels, something that clearly was not happening in the present. So even before we arrive at 1 Corinthians 15 Paul already indicated that the kingdom is future.

As 1 Cor 4:8 and 6:2–3 reveal, a close connection exists between the kingdom reign of Messiah and the reign of those who belong to Messiah. So if Paul clearly places the kingdom reign of the saints in the future (which he does) in 1 Cor 4:8 and 6:2–3, this makes it likely that the kingdom reign of the Son described in 1 Cor 15:20–28 is future as well. What Paul revealed earlier in 1 Corinthians helps inform what he is claiming later. Hence, both grammar and context indicate a futuristic understanding of Jesus' reign in 1 Corinthians 15.

Glorification and the Kingdom (1 Cor 15:50)

Paul spends much of his discussion after 1 Cor 15:20–28 on the nature and necessity of a physical resurrection of believers. He then returns to the topic of the kingdom in verse 50: "Now I say this, brethren, that flesh and blood cannot inherit the kingdom of God; nor does the perishable inherit the imperishable." This is not a claim that physical bodies do not exist in the kingdom of God or that believers are only spirits. He has already explicitly affirmed the resurrection of the body (see Rom 8:23). Instead, his point is that human beings in their fallen, perishable bodies cannot inherit God's imperishable glorious kingdom. One must be glorified to enter this kingdom.

Some, like Storms, claim this verse is inconsistent with premillennialism since it states that non-glorified people cannot inherit

God's kingdom. Allegedly this verse contradicts the view of premillennialism that Jesus' millennial kingdom will include those in non-glorified bodies (Isa 65:20).

So how does 1 Cor 15:50 relate to the kingdom? Paul already discussed the kingdom earlier in the chapter (see 1 Cor 15:20–28). He referred to two phases of the kingdom plan. First, there is a kingdom of Jesus, who must reign over the earth until all His enemies are defeated. After this, Jesus hands His kingdom over to the Father and the eternal kingdom commences. So what phase of the kingdom is Paul referring to in 15:50? *The Father's eternal kingdom, not Jesus' millennial kingdom, is probably in view.* Why? First, the Father's eternal kingdom after Jesus' kingdom has already been brought up in 1 Cor 15:24–28. And second, if the kingdom solely refers to Jesus' kingdom, the conditions Paul offers in verse 50 do not fit with other biblical truths, including the presence of childbirth and death (Isa 65:20). Nor does it fit with the conditions of Zechariah 14, where nations may still commit sin.

Third, all three millennial views require the kingdom of 15:50 to be the Father's eternal kingdom. Amillennialists and postmillennialists believe this age is the era for Jesus' millennial kingdom, but there is no glorification of believers in this age. If Paul is referring to Jesus' messianic/millennial kingdom in 15:50, then the amillennial and postmillennial views cannot be accurate either since those camps claim the millennium is in operation now and that Christians currently participate in Jesus' millennial kingdom in a non-glorified state. So it seems as if the other millennial views also need the reference to the kingdom in 1 Corinthians 15 to be a reference to the eternal kingdom of the Father as well. As Waymeyer observes:

> If the amillennialist insists that the two must be equated, then 1 Corinthians 15:50 presents an insurmountable obstacle for his own view as well, for this would require that believers today are part of the kingdom of God even though they have not yet been glorified. For this reason, 1 Corinthians 15:50 itself presents no more of a problem for premillennialism than it does for amillennialism.[14]

---

[14] Waymeyer, "A Biblical Critique of the Two-Age Model as an Argument against Premillennialism," 186.

Thus, one thing all three millennial views have in common is that Jesus' millennial kingdom includes non-glorified saints.

With 1 Cor 15:50 Paul is referring to the Father's eternal kingdom, or what we call the Eternal State. When it comes to the Father's eternal kingdom, everyone present must and will have glorified, imperishable bodies. So 1 Cor 15:50 is not evidence against premillennialism. It affirms that no one will enter God's eternal kingdom in a non-glorified body. Since all millennial views believe in a kingdom of Jesus where non-glorified bodies are present, this verse is no more of a challenge for premillennialism than for the other millennial views.

Does 1 Corinthians 15:51–57 Teach the Final Removal of Death at Jesus' Second Coming?

With 1 Cor 15:51–55 Paul explains the glorious truth that Christians will receive glorified bodies and experience the removal of death:

> Behold, I tell you a mystery; we will not all sleep, but we will all be changed, in a moment, in the twinkling of an eye, at the last trumpet; for the trumpet will sound, and the dead will be raised imperishable, and we will be changed. For this perishable must put on the imperishable, and this mortal must put on immortality. But DEATH, WHERE IS YOUR VICTORY? O DEATH, WHERE IS YOUR STING?" (1 Cor 15:51–55).

Storms argues that this passage makes premillennialism impossible since death allegedly is forever defeated with the return of Jesus. If death is finally removed as a result of Jesus' return, then how can death's final defeat occur a thousand years later as premillennialists claim?

The answer is linked with a correct understanding of what Paul stated earlier in 1 Cor 15:20–28 where he laid out a three-stage resurrection program. It must be noted that the defeat of death occurs for all who are resurrected. But as Paul indicated, not all experience resurrection and the defeat of death at the same time. For instance, Jesus' resurrection was the first phase of the resurrection program— "Christ the firstfruits." When Jesus rose from the dead He personally experienced the final removal of death. Concerning Jesus, Peter declared, "But God raised Him up again, putting an end to the agony of death, since it was impossible for Him to be held in its power." (Acts 2:24). Yet Jesus' triumph over death does not mean that death itself was finally removed for all time at that time. Nor does it mean there are no more phases of the resurrection program. Likewise, with 2 Tim 1:10 Paul said Jesus "abolished death and brought life and immortality to light through the gospel." Again, we could say "Jesus abolished death so there is no more death after this point." But that would not be accurate. We don't pit this verse against others that indicate other stages in the resurrection program.

Yes, the Corinthians (and all believers in this age) are destined to be resurrected in connection with the second stage of the resurrection program. In the twinkling of an eye they will go from mortality to immortality. For them death is removed at the second stage. But this does not mean there will not be a third stage of resurrection to come. *To summarize, with 1 Cor 15:51–57 Paul explains how the resurrection plan relates to his readers.* Since the believing Corinthians trusted in Christ, they will be part of the second phase of the resurrection plan—"those who are Christ's at His coming" (1 Cor 15:23b). For them, the removal of death will take place and they "will be changed" (15:51b) and for them "this perishable must put on the imperishable" (15:53a). Just as death was defeated for Jesus around A.D. 33, so too will death be defeated for those who experience Jesus' resurrection at His return. But this does not rule out a final stage of resurrection and the removal of death at the end of the millennium. This coincides with Rev 20:4b-5 in which a coming to life of martyred saints is followed by another resurrection *after* a thousand years are completed:

> and they [martyrs] came to life and reigned with Christ for a thousand years. The rest of the dead did not come to life until the thousand years were completed.

The best approach is not to appeal to 1 Cor 15:51–57 to show that Rev 20:4b–5 is not really teaching what is appears to teach. The correct approach is to see 1 Corinthians 15 and Revelation 20 as harmonizing with each other. Both reveal a gap of time between a physical resurrection at the time of Jesus' return and a physical resurrection for another group at the end of Jesus' kingdom reign. Waymeyer sees these passages as harmonizing when he states:

> The most plausible way to harmonize 1 Corinthians 15:51–57 with Revelation 20 is to see the language of victory over death in this passage as applicable to each stage of resurrection set forth in Scripture. According to this view, verses 51–53 do indeed describe the glorification of believers at the return of Christ, but this transformation of God's people does not signify the final destruction of death as an enemy which is able to claim lives. Instead, when the saints are glorified at the return of Christ, they themselves experience this victory over death as they are clothed with immortality, but the final destruction of death itself remains future, taking place when death and Hades are cast into the Lake of Fire at the end of the millennium (Rev 20:14; cf. 21:4).[15]

Conclusion

First Corinthians 15 is consistent with premillennialism. Not only does a proper understanding of this passage reveal a three-stage resurrection program that allows for a millennial reign of Jesus before the Eternal State, it refutes the claims of those who believe this passage is evidence against premillennialism. It is also remarkably similar to Rev 20:4–5 which explicitly teaches a millennial reign of Jesus and the saints between the return of Jesus and resurrection of the saints and the beginning of the eternal kingdom.

---

[15] Waymeyer, 187.

10

ANSWERING OBJECTIONS
TO PREMILLENNIALISM

Our purpose in this book has been to focus on a positive case for premillennialism. Here we address objections that are sometimes made against this view.

Objection: The case for premillennialism rests solely on Revelation 20, so we should not base our views of the millennium on just one passage.

Answer: First, this objection that premillennialism is only based on one passage is not true. But before we answer it we need to affirm that the Bible only has to address an issue once for it to be true. If Revelation 20 were the only passage that affirmed premillennialism that is still enough reason to believe it, particularly when the purpose of the book is prophecy and it clearly places a millennial kingdom (Revelation 20) between the return of Jesus (Revelation 19) and the Eternal State (Revelation 21).

Second, the basis for a coming earthly kingdom of man is found in Gen 1:26–28 where man is tasked to rule from and over the earth. Also, the Bible reveals a time period different from both our present age and the Eternal State. Passages like Isa 65:17–25; Zechariah 8; and Zechariah 14 best fit an intermediate era between these other two eras. Plus, the Bible also indicates that Messiah's earthly kingdom follows global tribulation, cosmic signs, rescue of God's people, and judgment for God's enemies. This is what we find in Revelation 19–20. Also, Isa 24:21–22 predicts a significant period of time consistent with a millennial kingdom when it said that evil spiritual and human forces would be imprisoned in a pit and "after many days they will be punished." The "after many days" points to a two-phased judgment that is very similar to what John describes in regard to the millennium in Rev 20:4–5. What was hinted at in the Old Testament became explicit with Revelation 20. As Wayne Grudem puts it:

> Similarly, in several of the Old and New Testament books leading up to the time of the writing of Revelation, there are *hints* of a future earthly millennium prior to the Eternal State, but the explicit teaching about it was left until John wrote Revelation. Since Revelation is the New Testament book that most explicitly teaches about things yet future, it is appropriate that this more explicit revelation of the future millennium would be put at this point in the Bible.[1]

The premillennial view of Revelation 20 finds support in earlier Bible passages. What is unique about Revelation 20 is that it tells us *how long* this intermediate kingdom will be—a thousand years.

Objection: Premillennialism is questionable because it is based on an obscure and symbolic book (Revelation) that is hard to understand and should not be taken literally.

Answer: Be careful when it comes to labeling something as "obscure." Revelation is not as obscure as some claim. The book is full of symbols, but most of them are either explained in the book or the symbolism can be understood from other Bible passages. Also, Jesus announced blessing upon those who study this book and heed what it says. There is no blessing promised for avoiding or downplaying its significance. No one is claiming that Revelation is always easy to interpret, but we need to take Revelation seriously and not downplay its importance. This is the last inspired revelation given to man in the Bible, and the Lord pronounced a blessing upon those who read

---

[1] Wayne Grudem, *Systematic Theology: An Introduction to Biblical Doctrine* (Grand Rapids: Zondervan, 1994), 1117.

and heed its significance. The last chapters of the last book of the Bible should be studied diligently. Also, Revelation is one of the few books in the Bible where we are told its genre, which is prophecy. The purpose of prophecy is to reveal events to come. The millennium of Revelation 20 comes within an identifiable literary section of Rev 19:11–21:8 that has chronological markers (*kai eidon*) that indicate sequence of events. There are good reasons to believe that the millennial kingdom of Revelation follows the second coming of Jesus in chapter 19 yet comes before the Eternal State of chapter 21.

Objection: Premillennialism says that people will sin and rebel against Jesus after His second coming, but it does not seem right that people could sin after Jesus returns.

Answer: This objection is based on the assumption that the return of Jesus must mean perfect conditions right away. But we must base our views of the future on what the Bible says, not on pre-understandings of how we think things should be. While some consider it unthinkable that sin and death could occur after Jesus returns, the Bible indicates this will happen. The Bible says that the Messiah must reign over His enemies (see 1 Cor 15:25) and that He will rule with a rod of iron (Rev 12:5; 19:15). Also, Jesus promises the church ruling functions with a rod of iron when He returns (see Rev 2:26–27). Ruling over enemies and ruling with a rod of iron seems to indicate a negative aspect of this rule. Isaiah 65:20 indicates that death may occur during this time period when long life is the norm. Isaiah 2:4 reveals that the Messiah will be settling disputes among the nations. Plus, Rev 20:7–10 explicitly states that a Satan-inspired rebellion will occur against the beloved city of Jerusalem after the thousand-year reign of the Messiah. This is a sinful rebellion that is squashed with destruction from God.

Yes the premillennialist acknowledges the presence of some sin and death during the millennium after Jesus' return, but this will reveal how a righteous ruler deals with sin. Sin is met with perfect justice. Also, compare the presence of sin and death with the millennial kingdom of amillennialism and postmillennialism. If the millennium is taking place in this present age, as those camps claim, rampant sin and rebellion occurs in Jesus' kingdom to a degree far greater than what the premillennialist posits. This present age is dominated with sin, rebellion, and death. Plus, no nation on earth bows the knee to

Jesus as Lord and Messiah. Conditions in this alleged millennial age are far worse than what the premillennialist believes will happen in the coming millennium. With the premillennial scenario, the world is drastically changed for the better and whatever sin occurs is met with swift and righteous judgment. This is far better than the millennium of amillennialism which allows for a millennial reign of Christ with continued rampant defiance against God and billions of people who do not even acknowledge the God of the Bible.

In addition, what the Bible says must trump how we think matters should be. Judgment of sin in connection with the millennium is taught in the Bible and is a way for the reigning Christ to bring glory to himself by squashing any challenges to His authority. Once the Eternal State begins we are told that sin and death will never occur again, so that day is coming. But in the intermediate kingdom of the millennium, sin and death can occur, but perfect justice is handed out by the reigning King.

Objection: Premillennialism allows for Jesus to be visibly reigning on the earth as King, yet there are many unbelievers who have not believed in Jesus. How can unbelievers exist in Jesus' kingdom?

Answer: This objection is against the premillennial view that unbelievers will be born and live their lives in the millennium. Premillennialists affirm this since there must be a nucleus of rebellious people who are part of the Satanic rebellion against the beloved city at the end of the millennium (see Rev 20:7–9).

Yes, unbelievers will exist in the millennium. They are part of the Messiah's reign over His enemies and His rule with a rod of iron. The language of ruling over enemies and ruling with a rod of iron indicates a negative aspect of the rule. This language does not describe the present age or the Eternal State, so it fits best with a millennial kingdom after the return of Jesus but before the Eternal State.

It may seem incredible to some that some people can see Jesus in person and still not believe. But was that not also the case at Jesus' first coming? Yes, Jesus' glory is more on display in the millennium, but most rejected Jesus at His first coming despite the incredible, miraculous works that He did. We also wonder why Satan and the angels who followed Him rebelled against God when they had perfect access to God. Sin has always been more of a heart issue than an intellectual issue. Satan may be the most intelligent being in the universe after God, yet he foolishly chose to rebel. It may be the case that the millennial reign of Christ further shows the sinfulness of unbelieving man. Even under ideal conditions with Satan and his activities totally absent, man still sins against God.

It also should be noted that amillennialism and postmillennialism have sin as part of their millennial scenarios. If the millennium is occurring in this age, there is far more sin and rebellion in Jesus' kingdom than what the premillennialist says will occur in a future earthly kingdom.

Objection: Premillennialism insists that there will be a rebellion of the nations at the end of the millennium, according to Rev 20:7–10, but Rev 19:18 indicates that all unbelievers are destroyed with the second coming of Jesus. So where does the rebellion come from if the nations against Christ have already been destroyed?

Answer: The rebellion of Rev 20:7–10 comes over a thousand years after the events of Revelation 19. Therefore, the nucleus for the rebellion at the end of the millennium probably comes from the progeny of those who entered the kingdom in non-glorified bodies. The millennial kingdom begins with only believers in Jesus, since judgment guarantees that no unbelievers inherit the kingdom initially (see Matt 25:31–46), but as procreation continues, the presence of those who have yet to believe in Jesus increases. After one-thousand years of peaceful conditions and no infant mortality,[2] the number of people, including those who have not yet trusted in Jesus, is probably quite large. Perhaps the number of unbelievers increases rapidly near the end of the thousand years. But either way, it is those born during this era that have never trusted Christ who will join the Satan-led rebellion that is immediately consumed by God.

Also, not every person on the planet is killed at the end of Revelation 19. The focus is on those involved with the Battle of Armageddon. Those who opposed Christ at this battle are all destroyed, but not every person on earth. In the parallel passage of Zechariah 14 the international siege of Jerusalem is thwarted by the returning Jesus who comes to the Mount of Olives and establishes His kingdom over the entire earth (Zech 14:3–4, 9). Yet Zech 14:16 then

---

[2] Isaiah 65:20 states: "No longer will there be in it an infant who lives but a few days."

speaks of nations after this who did not go up against Jerusalem: "Then it will come about *that any who are left of all the nations that went against Jerusalem* will go up from year to year to worship the King, the LORD of hosts, and to celebrate the Feast of Booths" (emphases mine). This shows that not all are killed with the event of Jesus' second coming.

Objection: The claim of premillennialists that people in glorified bodies co-exist in the same realm as those in non-glorified bodies is hard to believe.

Answer: Again, we have to make sure that we are not rejecting something simply because it seems implausible or not in line with how we think matters should be. The millennial kingdom is an intermediate kingdom that is both distinct and similar to the present age and the Eternal State in certain ways. It should not surprise us that an intermediate kingdom may have a mixture of conditions from each era. The millennium is far better than the present age but not perfect like the Eternal State. Why could it not be the case that there is a mixture of those who have glorified and non-glorified bodies? The resurrected Jesus was present for forty days with His non-glorified disciples. When Jesus died, resurrected saints walked the streets of Jerusalem (see Matt 27:52–53). Plus, while glorified bodies are certainly superior to non-glorified bodies since they are not subject to death or decay, their spatial dimensions are probably similar to non-glorified bodies. The glorified Jesus seemed normal to those He encountered on the road to Emmaus after His resurrection. He probably did not appear 20-feet tall with a halo on His head. Adam's pre-Fall dimensions and appearance were probably not radically different from post-Fall bodies that people had, although those bodies were now subject to decay and death.

Objection: The New Testament indicates that there are two ages—a present age and an age to come. There is no indication of a transitional millennial age.

Answer: Just as this present age can have multiple eras or dispensations such as (1) pre-Fall/post-Fall; (2) pre-Flood/post-Flood; and (3) Old Covenant era/New Covenant era, so too can the "age to come" contain multiple phases to it—a millennial kingdom phase followed by an eternal kingdom phase. In Eph 2:7, Paul refers to "ages to come" (plural) in which God's grace will be manifested to believers. One of these "ages" could be a millennial kingdom phase.

The amillennialist, Geerhardus Vos, rightly declared that premillennialists should have no objection to the immediate succession of the two ages, because "under their scheme the millennium could in part be identified with the age to come as the beginning thereof."[3] In other words, the millennium could operate as the first phase of the age to come. In his evaluation of Vos's statement, Matthew Waymeyer observes, "For this reason, Vos, unlike other amillennialists, did not see the immediate succession of the two ages as necessarily excluding an intermediate kingdom between the present age and the Eternal State."[4] Thus, the millennium will function as the initial phase of the "age to come."

Objection: The view that the events of Rev 19:11–21:8 are sequential is refuted by the fact that recapitulation is occurring in Revelation. For example, the binding of Satan described in Rev 20:1–3 is describing the same battle as Revelation 12.

Answer: This objection assumes that the presence of similarities with events means sameness. But similarities do not always mean sameness. Yes, there are similarities between Rev 20:1–3 and Revelation 12. Both describe a spiritual battle that involves Satan and angels with Satan being cast down. But the striking distinctions indicate that these passages are describing different battles at different time periods. Compare:

There are two different *destinies*:

> Rev 12: Satan is cast from heaven to earth.
> Rev 20: Satan is cast from earth to the abyss (which allows no access to earth).

---

[3] Geerhardus Vos, *The Pauline Eschatology*, (P & R Publishing Company, 1979), 25.

[4] Matthew William Waymeyer, "A Biblical Critique of the Two-Age Model as an Argument against Premillennialism," Ph.D. diss., The Master's Seminary, 2015, 101, n. 45.

There are two different *results*:

> Rev 12: Satan being cast to earth results in more deception of the nations.
> Rev 20: Satan's binding results in a cessation of deceiving the nations.

There are two different *time periods*:

> Rev 12: Satan knows his time is short ("he has only a short time").
> Rev 20: Satan is bound for a long time ("thousand years").

Like many battles throughout human history, the cosmic battle between God and Satan is a prolonged war with several different battles. The significant differences between the battles of Revelation 12 and 20 rule out the possibility that they are referring to the same event.

Objection: The Bible teaches the final removal of death at the time of Jesus' second coming, not a thousand years after His return.

Answer: This objection was answered in our chapter on 1 Corinthians 15 so I recommend going back to this chapter. But in short, the Bible teaches that death is not removed entirely until the end of the millennium, which occurs a thousand years after Jesus' second coming. Remember the chronology: Revelation 19:11–21 speaks of the second coming of Jesus. Then Rev 20:1–6 speaks of a first resurrection and the reign of Jesus' saints. Then Rev 20:7–10 speaks of a Satan-led rebellion after the thousand years. Then Rev 20:11–15 speaks of the wicked and death itself being thrown into the lake of fire. This second resurrection was explicitly stated to occur a thousand years after the first resurrection in Rev 20:4b–5. So Revelation 19 and 20 tells of death after Jesus' return.

First Corinthians 15:20–24 speaks of a three-stage resurrection program: (1) Christ the firstfruits; (2) after that those who are Christ's at His coming; and (3) then the end. The end occurs between phases 2 and 3 when Christ reigns over His enemies and abolishes death (1 Cor 15:25–26). The non-premillennialist does not accept

this understanding, but this understanding is reasonable and proba-
ble, and is evidence that death is not finally removed until sometime
after Jesus' second coming. The removal of death is part of the task
of Jesus' mediatorial reign over earth.

Also, Isa 65:20 speaks of rare but premature death during new
earth conditions (Isa 65:17). While not explicitly mentioning death,
Zechariah 14 speaks of severe consequences for the nations that dis-
obey God after Jesus returned to the Mount of Olives and is King
over all the earth (Zech 14:4, 9, 16–19).

Finally, 1 Cor 15:51–57 is not a defeater for premillennialism
since what Paul is emphasizing here is the defeat of death for his
Corinthian readers who will be part of the second phase of the resurrection program—"those who are Christ's at His coming" (1 Cor
15:23). But this does not mean death is entirely removed from the
cosmos at this point any more than Jesus' abolishing of death with
His first coming meant death was finally removed for all time then
(2 Tim 1:10). The contexts of these passages and the Bible's storyline
must be considered.

Conclusion

There are other objections against premillennialism than those
mentioned here. Each view of the millennium has its own problems
or difficult passages to grapple with. But overall premillennialism has
less problems than the other millennial views.

Most of the objections against premillennialism are in the
"doesn't seem likely" category rather than true contradictions or
problems. Arguments such as "It doesn't seem right that there
should be sin or unbelievers in the millennium," or "It seems weird
that glorified and non-glorified people would co-exist together," are
not true problems for premillennialism. They certainly are relevant
issues to discuss and debate, but they do not overturn the premillennial view. On the other hand, there are several issues that seem to
demand premillennialism:

If the events of Revelation 20 follow the events of Revelation
19 chronologically, then premillennialism must be true.

If the two resurrections of Rev 20:4–5 are physical resurrections (which all admit the second is physical), then premillennialism must be true.

If the abyss in which Satan is thrown is a real spiritual prison where he as a person is incarcerated, then premillennialism must be true (Rev 20:1–3).

If Jesus assumes His Davidic throne at the time of His second coming as Matt 19:28 and Matt 25:31 indicate, then Jesus' kingdom is future from our standpoint and premillennialism must be true.

If the successful reign of the Last Adam and mankind must take place from and over the realm where God originally placed and tasked the first Adam, then premillennialism must be true.

If all of the covenants and promises of the Bible must be fulfilled in all their dimensions (spiritual and physical; national and international) under the Messiah before the Eternal State begins, then premillennialism must be true.

CONCLUSION

Premillennialism is the view that there will be an intermediate kingdom of a thousand years after this present age and before the Eternal State. This work has offered a case for premillennialism by offering: (1) scriptural support for this view from both the Old and New Testaments and (2) a rationale why premillennialism is necessary and strategic to the Bible's storyline.

Genesis 1:26–28 is the foundation for the idea of a successful earthly reign of man for the glory of God. It affirms that God's plan is for man to rule from earth over the earth. God did not create man to rule from heaven or over heaven (Ps 115:16). Premillennialism gets these truths right. Plus, Old Testament passages such as Psalm 2; 110; Isaiah 2; 9; 11; 65; Daniel 2; Zechariah 8; 14 teach a coming earthly kingdom of the Messiah.

Isaiah 24:21–22 is a precursor for the intermediate kingdom of Revelation 20 since it speaks of a gap of "many days" between the imprisonment of wicked human and spiritual forces and their final punishment. This is exactly what occurs in Revelation 19–20. Also, various Old Testament passages tell of a time that is much better than our present age yet not perfect like the coming Eternal State. Passages like Isa 65:17–25; Psalm 72; and Zechariah 8 and 14 teach this. In addition, several New Testament passages present the reign and rule of the kingdom as future (Acts 1:6), and the Davidic throne of Jesus being established with Jesus' second coming (Matt 19:28; 25:31; 2 Tim 2:12; Rev 5:10).

Then there is Revelation 20 with its explicit discussion of a kingdom that is a thousand years long (Rev 20:1–10). This kingdom comes after the second coming of Jesus (Rev 19:11ff.) but before the Eternal State (Rev 21:1–22:5).

The rationale for premillennialism was found in the following points:

1. There must be a successful reign of man and the Last Adam (Jesus) *from* and *over* the realm where God tasked the first Adam to rule.

2. Jesus must have a sustained and visible reign in the realm where He was rejected.

3. There must be a vindication and reign of the saints in the realm where they were persecuted.

4. There needs to be a time in history in which all aspects of the biblical covenants and promises are fulfilled.

Also, premillennialism consistently affirms the goodness of God's physical creation against all forms of Platonism. The original creation was "very good," and even with the Fall God does not give up on His creation. He plans to regenerate and restore it (Matt 19:28; Acts 3:21).

These points reveal that premillennialism is important. It has implications for the Christian worldview and the Messiah's role in it. The correct view of the millennium is that of premillennialism.

RECOMMENDED WORKS
ON PREMILLENNIALISM

Benware, Paul N. *Understanding End Times Prophecy: A Comprehensive Approach.* Chicago: Moody, 2006.

Blaising, Craig A., "Premillennialism," in *Three Views on the Millennium and Beyond,* ed. Darrell L. Bock. Grand Rapids: Zondervan, 1999, 157–227.

Campbell, Donald K. and Jeffrey L. Townsend, eds. *The Coming Millennial Kingdom: A Case for Premillennial Interpretation.* Grand Rapids: Kregel, 1997.

MacArthur, John and Richard Mayhue. *Christ's Prophetic Plans: A Futuristic Premillennial Primer.* Chicago: Moody, 2012.

McClain, Alva J. *The Greatness of the Kingdom: An Inductive Study of the Kingdom of God.* Winona Lake, IN: BMH, 2001.

Saucy, Robert L. *The Case for Progressive Dispensationalism: The Interface Between Dispensational and Non-Dispensational Theology.* Grand Rapids: Zondervan Publishing House, 1993.

Waymeyer, Matt. *Revelation 20 and the Millennial Debate.* Kress Christian Publications, 2004.

Made in United States
Orlando, FL
25 April 2024

46178173R00068